I0802397

JESUS' SPEECH ON THE MOUNT OF OLIVES

A 12-WEEK STUDY

Murray J. Smith

CROSSWAY®

WHEATON, ILLINOIS

Knowing the Bible: Jesus' Speech on the Mount of Olives, A 12-Week Study

Published by Crossway
1300 Crescent Street
Wheaton, Illinois 60187

Cover design: Simplicated Studio

First printing 2025

Printed in the United States of America

All emphases in Scripture quotations have been added by the author.

Trade paperback ISBN: 978-1-4335-9502-8

EPub ISBN: 978-1-4335-9504-2
PDF ISBN: 978-1-4335-9503-5

Crossway is a publishing ministry of Good News Publishers.

VP 35 34 33 32 31 30 29 28 27 26 25
15 14 13 12 11 10 9 8 7 6 5 4 3 2 1

KNOWING THE BIBLE

Douglas Sean O'Donnell, Series Editor

• • • • • •

Genesis
Exodus
Leviticus
Numbers
Deuteronomy
Joshua
Judges
Ruth and Esther
1–2 Samuel
1–2 Kings
1–2 Chronicles
Ezra and Nehemiah
Job
Psalms
Proverbs

Ecclesiastes
Song of Solomon
Isaiah
Jeremiah
Lamentations, Habakkuk, and Zephaniah
Ezekiel
Daniel
Hosea
Joel, Amos, and Obadiah
Jonah, Micah, and Nahum
Haggai, Zechariah, and Malachi
Matthew
Mark
Luke
John

Acts
Romans
1 Corinthians
2 Corinthians
Galatians
Ephesians
Philippians
Colossians and Philemon
1–2 Thessalonians
1–2 Timothy and Titus
Hebrews
James
1–2 Peter and Jude
1–3 John
Revelation

The Ten Commandments
The Miracles of Jesus
The Parables of Jesus
Jesus' Speech on the Mount of Olives
The Sermon on the Mount
Jesus' Farewell Discourse

• • • • • •

DOUGLAS SEAN O'DONNELL (PhD, University of Aberdeen) is the Senior Vice President of Bible Editorial at Crossway. He is the author and editor of more than a dozen books, including *The Beginning and End of Wisdom*; *The Pastor's Book*; *The Song of Solomon* and *Matthew* in the Preaching the Word commentary series; and *Psalms* and *The Parables of Jesus* in the Knowing the Bible series. He also contributed *Song of Solomon* and *Job* to the ESV Expository Commentary.

"This series is a tremendous resource for those wanting to study and teach the Bible with an understanding of how the gospel is woven throughout Scripture. Here are gospel-minded pastors and scholars doing gospel business from all the Scriptures. This is a biblical and theological feast preparing God's people to apply the entire Bible to all of life with heart and mind wholly committed to Christ's priorities."

BRYAN CHAPELL, pastor; author, *Christ-Centered Preaching* and *Christ-Centered Worship*

"Mark Twain may have smiled when he wrote to a friend, 'I didn't have time to write you a short letter, so I wrote you a long letter.' But the truth of Twain's remark remains serious and universal, because well-reasoned, compact writing requires extra time and extra hard work. And this is what we have in the Crossway Bible study series *Knowing the Bible.* The skilled authors and notable editors provide the contours of each book of the Bible as well as the grand theological themes that bind them together as one Book. Here, in a 12-week format, are carefully wrought studies that will ignite the mind and the heart."

R. KENT HUGHES, Senior Pastor Emeritus, College Church, Wheaton, Illinois

"*Knowing the Bible* brings together a gifted team of Bible teachers to produce a high-quality series of study guides. The coordinated focus of these materials is unique: biblical content, provocative questions, systematic theology, practical application, and the gospel story of God's grace presented all the way through Scripture."

PHILIP G. RYKEN, President, Wheaton College

"These *Knowing the Bible* volumes provide a significant and very welcome variation on the general run of inductive Bible studies. This series provides substantial instruction, as well as teaching through the very questions that are asked. *Knowing the Bible* then goes even further by showing how any given text links with the gospel, the whole Bible, and the formation of theology. I heartily endorse this orientation of individual books to the whole Bible and the gospel, and I applaud the demonstration that sound theology was not something invented later by Christians, but is right there in the pages of Scripture."

GRAEME L. GOLDSWORTHY, former lecturer in Old Testament, Biblical Theology, and Hermeneutics, Moore Theological College

"What a gift to earnest, Bible-loving, Bible-searching believers! The organization and structure of the Bible study format presented through the *Knowing the Bible* series is so well conceived. Students of the Word are led to understand the content of passages through perceptive, guided questions, and they are given rich insights and application all along the way in the brief but illuminating sections that conclude each study. What potential growth in depth and breadth of understanding these studies offer! One can only pray that vast numbers of believers will discover more of God and the beauty of his Word through these rich studies."

BRUCE A. WARE, T. Rupert and Lucille Coleman Professor of Christian Theology, The Southern Baptist Theological Seminary

TABLE OF CONTENTS

SERIES PREFACE

KNOWING THE BIBLE, as the title indicates, was created to help readers know and understand the meaning, the message, and the God of the Bible. This series was created and edited by Lane Dennis and Dane Ortlund, and J. I. Packer served as the theological editor. Dr. Packer has gone to be with the Lord, Lane has retired as CEO and president of Crossway, and Dane now serves as senior pastor of Naperville (Illinois) Presbyterian Church. We are so grateful for their labors in overseeing the first forty-plus volumes of this series! To honor and expand upon their idea, we are continuing the series, focusing on key sections from Scripture, such as the Ten Commandments and the Sermon on the Mount.

Each volume in the series consists of twelve units that progressively take the reader through a clear, concise, and deep study of certain portions of Scripture. The material works best for a small group, as the questions are designed for good interactive group discussion. Even so, an individual could easily use the material for a personal Bible study as well.

Week 1 provides an overview of the section or sections of Scripture to be studied, which includes placing the text into its larger context (e.g., the Sermon on the Mount within the Gospel of Matthew), providing key historical background, and offering some questions to get started. Weeks 2–12 each have the following features: a summary of how the text fits into the rest of Scripture ("The Place of the Passage"), a summary sentence on the main theme ("The Big Picture"), and ten or so questions ("Reflection and Discussion Questions"). Moreover, each unit highlights the role of the gospel of grace in each text ("Gospel Glimpses"), identifies whole-Bible themes ("Whole-Bible Connections"), pinpoints Christian doctrines ("Theological Soundings"), defines key terms ("Definitions"), and allows space to respond ("Personal Implications").

Lastly, to help readers understand the Bible better, we urge readers to use the ESV Bible and the *ESV Study Bible*, which are available in various print and digital formats, including online editions at esv.org. The *Knowing the Bible* series is also available online.

May our gracious God, who has generously given his Spirit and his Word, use this study to grow his people in their knowledge and love of the Father, Son, and Spirit.

Douglas Sean O'Donnell
Series Editor

Week 1: Overview

Getting Acquainted

In his speech on the Mount of Olives our Lord looks to the future to give his people hope. He speaks prophetically of events that will occur within a generation and—beyond that—promises his own return in glory at the end of the age. The speech is often called the "Olivet Discourse" because Jesus "sat on the Mount of Olives" when he spoke these words (Matt. 24:3 // Mark 13:3). It appears in each of the three Synoptic Gospels[1], toward the end of Jesus' life (Matt. 24–25; Mark 13; Luke 21). Knowing that his death, resurrection, and ascension are near (Matt. 16:21; Mark 8:31; Luke 9:22), Jesus now prepares his disciples for the end. In this speech he teaches them—and us—how to live faithfully in the period between his resurrection and his return.

In these studies we will focus on Jesus' speech as recorded in the Gospel of Matthew. In Weeks 2–9 we will work our way through each section of the speech in Matthew 24–25. In Weeks 10–11 we will study Jesus' speech in the Gospels of Mark (Mark 13) and Luke (Luke 21). In Week 12 we will see how the apostles apply Jesus' speech in their letters and in the book of Revelation.

In this first study our goal is to gain an overview of Jesus' speech. You will undoubtedly still have questions at the end, but we ought to avoid getting bogged down in the details at this point. Our goal for now is to take in the big picture as Jesus lifts our eyes to God's promised future.

Placing It in the Larger Story

Jesus' speech on the Mount of Olives is a crucial and encouraging part of God's Word, but it is also complex and controversial. The speech has been interpreted in three main ways.

PRETERIST: Preterist interpreters (from the Latin *praeter* = "past") hold that the whole of Jesus' speech in Matthew 24:4–35 refers to events in the first century. Jesus especially warns his disciples of God's judgment coming on Jerusalem and its temple (24:15–28). His prophecy of the "coming Son of Man" (24:29–31) is not about a different future event (his second coming) but refers metaphorically to the same "earth-shattering" events of the first century.

Partial Preterists recognize that Jesus does speak of his second coming in Matthew 24:36–25:46 and that the New Testament elsewhere promises his return. Full Preterism, which denies the second coming altogether, is an unbiblical heresy.

FUTURIST: Futurist interpreters hold that the whole of Jesus' speech refers to events that even now remain in the future. On this view Jesus prophesies events that will follow the future "rapture" of the church, although most futurists believe that he does not speak of that event here. His focus is on the people of national/ethnic Israel, who will suffer increased difficulty and persecution before and/or during the "great tribulation" (24:21). The nations will gather for battle against Jerusalem, leading to the destruction of the rebuilt temple (24:15–28). Finally, the Lord himself will come from heaven with power and great glory (24:29–31).

INAUGURATED: The most common interpretation, and the one followed here, sees that Jesus speaks *both* of events facing his disciples in the first century *and also* of the whole period of gospel mission to the nations before his final return in glory at the end. This recognizes that Jesus' speech holds out an inaugurated eschatology.[2] In Jesus' life, death, resurrection, and gift of the Spirit, God has inaugurated the final stage of redemptive history. We are living now, already, in "the last days" (Acts 2:17; Heb. 1:2), while we also wait in hope for the "end of the age" (Matt. 13:39–40, 49; 24:3; 28:20) when Jesus will return (10:23; 16:27; 19:28; 24:30; 25:31; 26:64).

The outline below shows how Jesus first answers the disciples' question (24:3) by telling them *what* to expect: he surveys the whole period between his present and the end (24:4–31) and prophesies both God's judgment on Jerusalem (24:15–21) and his own return in glory (24:29–31). Jesus next clarifies *when* these events will occur: Jerusalem will be destroyed within a generation (24:32–35), but no one knows when he will return (24:36–44). In the final part of the speech Jesus poses the question, "*Who* will be ready when he comes?" (24:45–25:46).

Throughout the whole speech Jesus is preparing his disciples—including us—to live for him in the present, to bear witness to him in all the world, and to be ready to meet him on the great final day.

Key Verse

"Therefore you also must be ready, for the Son of Man is coming at an hour you do not expect" (Matt. 24:44).

Date and Historical Background

The Gospel of Matthew was most likely written by Matthew (also known as Levi), a former tax collector who became one of the twelve apostles (see Matt. 9:9; 10:3). Matthew probably wrote his Gospel before the destruction of Jerusalem in AD 70. As a Galilean Jewish Christian and an apostle taught by Jesus (see 13:52; 28:20), he knew the Old Testament Scriptures well and was able to show how Jesus' words, actions, death, and resurrection "fulfill" them (e.g. 1:22–23; 12:17–21; 21:4–5).

Matthew wrote the Gospel to present Jesus as the Christ[3] and Son of God (1:1; 16:16), who came to establish God's kingdom and "save his people from their sins" (1:21; 4:17; 26:28). The Gospel has a Jewish flavor but shows concern for both the "lost sheep of the house of Israel" (10:6; 15:24) and all nations (24:14; 28:19). With its orderly presentation of Christ's ministry and breadth of ethical teaching (5:1–7:29), the Gospel serves as a basic course in discipleship for everyone who reads it (28:18–20).

Outline of Matthew 24–25

- **I. The Disciples' Question (24:1–3)**
- **II. Jesus' Answer (24:4–25:46)**
  - **A. What? (24:4–31)**
    - **1. From Now Until the End: Tribulation and Gospel Mission (24:4–28)**
      - **a. From Now Until the End: Falsehood, Falling Away, and Faithful Witness (24:4–14)**
      - **b. The Great Tribulation: Destruction of Jerusalem (24:15–21)**
      - **c. From Now until the End: Falsehood, Falling Away, Until the Son of Man Comes (24:22–28)**
    - **2. The End Itself: The Coming of the Son of Man (24:29–31)**

B. When? (24:32–44)

1. **Jerusalem Will Be Destroyed: Within a Generation! (24:32–35)**
2. **The Coming of the Son of Man: No One Knows! (24:36–44)**

C. Who Will Be Ready? (24:45–25:46)

1. **Faithful or Wicked Servants? (24:45–51)**
2. **Wise or Foolish Virgins? (25:1–13)**
3. **Shrewd or Slothful Servants? (25:14–30)**
4. **Sheep or Goats? (25:31–46)**

As You Get Started

After reading read the whole of Matthew 24–25, what general impressions do you have? Choose three words to summarize Jesus' teaching in this speech.

Jesus' location "on the Mount of Olives" (Matt. 24:3) recalls Zechariah's prophecy that the Lord will manifest his presence on the "Mount of Olives" when he comes to judge the nations and establish himself as "king over all the earth" (Zech. 14:1–9). How does this allusion to Zechariah shape our expectations for what Jesus' speech will be about?

In Matthew 24:3 the disciples come to Jesus as he sits on the mount overlooking the temple and ask him, "When will *these things* be, and what will be the sign of *your coming and of the end of the age*?" These questions provide a key to understanding the structure of Jesus' speech. In the immediate context (24:1–2), what are "these things"? When is the "end of the age"? (Look for this phrase in Matt. 13:36–43, 47–50; 28:18–20). How are "these things" and the "end of the age" distinguished from each other?

In Matthew 24:15–21 Jesus focuses on "these things" that will occur within a generation: the destruction of Jerusalem and its temple (cf. 24:1–2, 34). His prophecy is fulfilled in AD 70 when Roman armies surround Jerusalem, capture the city, destroy the temple, and kill or enslave its inhabitants. How does Jesus describe those events? How should his disciples respond? How will God show grace even amid great hardship?

Matthew 24:29–31 is the climax of Jesus' speech, as he promises his own return at the end of the age. How is this event both similar to and different from the destruction of Jerusalem (24:15–21)?

Focus on Matthew 24:32–44. Jesus now explains the timeline for the events he has prophesied. What are "all these things" that will take place within a generation? (Hint: look for similar phrases in 24:2–3, 8.) What is "that day and hour" about which "no one knows" (24:36)? (Hint: look back at 24:27, 29–31.)

In Matthew 25 Jesus tells the parables of the virgins (25:1–13) and the talents (25:14–30) and pictures the final judgment of the sheep and the goats (25:31–46). Each part is designed to help us prepare for Jesus' return. Choose one word for each part to summarize what it means to be ready for the final day.

As You Finish This Unit . . .

Take a moment now to ask for the Lord's blessing and help as you continue in this study of Jesus' speech on the Mount of Olives. As you reflect on Jesus' promises for the future and what they mean for the present, pray, especially, that the "God of hope" might "fill you with all joy and peace in believing, so that by the power of the Holy Spirit you may abound in hope" (Rom. 15:13).

Definitions

[1] **Synoptic Gospels** – "Synoptic" comes from the Greek syn-opsis and means "seeing together." The Gospels of Matthew, Mark, and Luke are referred to as the Synoptic Gospels because they present Jesus' life, death, and resurrection from a similar perspective.

[2] **Eschatology** – The study of "the end" or "the last things" from Greek word *eschatos*, which means "last" or "final." Biblical eschatology concerns God's plans and promises for the "end" or "goal" of his creation.

[3] **Christ** – The English word "Christ" (Matt. 24:5, 23) comes from the Greek *Christos*, which itself translates the Hebrew *mashiach* ("Messiah"). Both terms—"Christ" and "Messiah"—mean "anointed." In the Old Testament period, prophets (e.g., 1 Kings 19:16; Ps. 105:15), priests (e.g., Ex. 29:7; Lev. 4:3, 5), and especially kings (e.g., 1 Sam. 16:13; Ps. 2:2) were anointed to indicate their appointment to office. In the New Testament, beginning in the Gospels, Jesus is declared "the Christ" (e.g., Matt. 1:1, 16–18; 16:16)—the end-time prophet, priest, and king, whom God has "anointed" to bring judgment and salvation.

WEEK 2: THE TIMELINE OF HISTORY

"ALL THESE THINGS" BEFORE "THE END"

Matthew 24:3–14

The Place of the Passage

Throughout Matthew Jesus announces the gospel[1] of God's coming kingdom (4:17, 23; 9:35; 24:14). He also warns that those who reject God's reign will face God's righteous judgment. Jesus speaks of this judgment against a double horizon: Within a generation, it will come on Jesus' contemporaries in the land of Israel (12:43–45; 21:43, 45; 23:34–36); ultimately, it will come at "the end of the age" on all people everywhere (7:21–23; 12:39–42; 13:36–43, 47–50; 19:28; 25:31–46). As we now begin to study in detail Jesus' discourse on the Mount of Olives, we will see that his answer to the disciples' question (24:3) shares this double horizon: Jesus speaks *both* of events that will occur within a generation (esp. 24:15–21) *and* of the whole period stretching out toward his return at the "end of the age" (esp. 24:4–14, 23–31). Our focus in this study is on the first part of Jesus' speech, wherein he surveys the whole period between his present and "the end," between his resurrection and his return (esp. 24:4–14).

The Big Picture

The period between Jesus' resurrection and return will be characterized by distress and difficulty, lies and lawlessness, falsehood and falling away. Those who belong to Jesus should not be surprised at this but should press on in bearing faithful witness to him, proclaiming the gospel to all nations until the end.

Reflection and Discussion

Read through the complete passage for this study, Matthew 24:3–14. Then think through and write your own notes on the following questions. (For further background see the *ESV Study Bible*, page 1873, or visit esv.org.)

As we saw last week, the disciples' question in Matthew 24:3 provides a key to the structure of Jesus' speech. Although the disciples may have conflated "these things" with the "end of the age," Jesus distinguishes the two. In verses 4–14 he begins his answer to the disciples' question by explaining what life will be like in the whole period between his present and the end of the age. What hardships does Jesus teach us to expect? How does Jesus give us hope amid these hardships?

In Matthew 24:8 Jesus explains that the events he prophesies in verses 4–7 are "but the beginning of the birth pains." How does this image of "birth pains" indicate both suffering and hope? Compare the use of the image in Romans 8:22–25. You can also look at Isaiah 26:17–19; 66:7–11; Micah 4:9–10; and John 16:20–22.

In Matthew 24:9 Jesus warns that his disciples "will be hated by all nations *for my name's sake.*" Read Matthew 1:21–25; 12:18–21; 18:18–20; and 28:16–20, which show the significance of Jesus' name. How do these passages encourage us to hold fast to his name, even if we are hated for it?

In Matthew 24:12 Jesus warns that "because lawlessness will be increased, the love of many will grow cold." How might lawlessness lead to lovelessness? How can we encourage each other to remain warm in our love for God and others (22:37–40) even amid increasing lawlessness?

In Matthew 24:13 Jesus promises that "the one who endures to the end will be saved" (note also "the end" in 24:6, 14). Does this refer to "the end" of a person's life, "the end of the age," or somehow both? How do verses 9–12 help us to understand what it means to endure in the Christian life? How can we help each other to endure in this way?

In Matthew 24:14 Jesus prophesies that "this gospel of the kingdom will be proclaimed throughout the whole world as a testimony to all nations, and then the end will come." Read Matthew 28:16–20. How does Jesus provide for this prophecy to be fulfilled? What further encouragements does he provide for the task?

As you have heard our Lord's teaching regarding life in this age—between his resurrection and his return—what is *one thing* you need to hold onto in the coming week?

Read through the following three sections on *Gospel Glimpses*, *Whole-Bible Connections*, and *Theological Soundings*. Then take time to consider the *Personal Implications* these sections have for you.

Gospel Glimpses

THE LORD WILL SAVE HIS PEOPLE. Jesus' promise in Matthew 24:13 reminds us of an important gospel truth: it is *God* who saves his people. Notice that Jesus does not say, "the one who endures to the end *will save himself*." He promises, rather, "the one who endures to the end *will be saved*." The passive voice is important. We call it a "divine passive" because it indicates that *God* is the one who saves us. This does not mean that we should abandon all responsibility in a misguided attempt to "let go and let God." We certainly need to endure by trusting in Christ, loving him and others, rejecting false saviors of every kind (24:4–5, 11), and playing our part in bearing witness to him (24:14). Ultimately, however, the same God who has provided for our salvation in Christ will also enable us, by the work of his Spirit, to keep trusting in Christ to the end, and so be saved.

Whole-Bible Connections

THIS MUST TAKE PLACE. Jesus' affirmation that "this must take place" (24:6) echoes God's word to King Nebuchadnezzar through the prophet Daniel, revealing "what will be in latter days" (Dan. 2:28–29, 45). In fact, Jesus' words in the following verses further echo Daniel's prophecies of kingdoms rising against kingdoms (Matt. 24:7; Dan. 7:23–24), of God's people's being persecuted (Matt. 24:9; Dan. 7:25), and of God's blessing the one who endures to the end (Matt. 24:13; Dan. 12:12). Jesus' words in the remainder of the speech include further echoes of the prophet Daniel (Matt. 24:15, 30). Both Daniel and Jesus affirm God's sovereign providence over history. The God of heaven *knows* the future and *reveals* the future because he has *planned* the future in advance. He "works all things according to the counsel of his will" (Eph. 1:11). This truth should give us deep confidence no matter what happens. For, although Jesus warns of difficult and troubling events that will test us and require endurance, we can know that God is at work, even in the most difficult circumstances, to bring about his perfect plan. We need not be "alarmed" when trials come (Matt. 24:6) but can take comfort in knowing that God will bring his people through every trial into his eternal kingdom and that "the one who endures to the end will be saved" (24:13).

Theological Soundings

THE GOSPEL MISSION WILL NOT FAIL. Jesus promises that the "gospel of the kingdom will be proclaimed throughout the whole world" and "then the end will come" (24:14). As we look back on the two thousand years since Jesus uttered these words, we can see how his prophecy has been progressively fulfilled, as the gospel has spread from Jerusalem, Judea, and Samaria to the ends of the earth (cf. Acts 1:8). In the vast tapestry of world history—a history full of wars, famines, earthquakes, and more—the single most significant thread has been the proclamation of the gospel throughout the world. The church's mission of bearing witness to Christ is not yet complete, and the church will suffer difficulties of all kinds, including persecution, until the end. But we have his promise that our mission will not fail. Wonderfully, while we each have a part to play, Jesus himself will ultimately ensure that the good news reaches the ends of the earth. As he says to Peter, "*I* will build *my* church, and the gates of hell shall not prevail against it" (Matt. 16:18). Jesus' promises should give the church confidence as we "go . . . and make disciples of all nations," knowing that he is with us "always, to the end of the age" (28:18–20).

Personal Implications

Take time to reflect on the implications of Matthew 24:3–14 for your own life today. Consider what you have learned that might lead you to praise God, repent of sin, and trust in his gracious promises. Make notes below on the personal implications for your walk with the Lord of the (1) *Gospel Glimpses*, (2) *Whole-Bible Connections*, (3) *Theological Soundings*, and (4) the passage as a whole.

1. Gospel Glimpses

2. Whole-Bible Connections

3. Theological Soundings

4. Matthew 24:3–14

As You Finish This Unit . . .

Take a moment now to ask for the Lord's blessing and help as you continue in this study of Jesus' speech on the Mount of Olives. As you reflect on Jesus' promises for the future and what they mean for the present, pray especially that the "God of hope" might "fill you with all joy and peace in believing, so that by the power of the Holy Spirit you may abound in hope" (Rom. 15:13).

Definitions

[1] **Gospel** – A common translation for a Greek word meaning "good news," that is, the good news of God's kingdom and the salvation he achieved though Jesus' life, death, and resurrection, which will be consummated when Jesus returns. *Gospel* with an initial capital letter refers to each of the biblical accounts of Jesus' life on earth (Matthew, Mark, Luke, and John).

Week 3: The Abomination of Desolation

The Judgment of Jerusalem and Beyond

Matthew 24:1–2, 15–28

The Place of the Passage

In Matthew 24:15–28 Jesus focuses on God's judgment falling on Jerusalem and its temple. This is a major theme of the Gospel of Matthew. In Galilee Jesus warns that those who do not receive him are like a "foolish man" whose "house" will come crashing down (7:26–27). In Jerusalem Jesus overturns the tables in the temple courts, prophetically enacting God's coming judgment (21:12–13). He tells parables about a vineyard owner and a king who bring judgment on the "tenants" and the "city" that refuse to honor the son (21:33–44; 22:1–7). He announces "woes" on the scribes and the Pharisees (23:1–36) and judgment on his own generation (12:41–42, 45; 23:36). He laments over Jerusalem, warning that its "house" is left "desolate" and its judgment will come soon (23:37–24:1). The destruction of Jerusalem was both God's judgment on his faithless people and the end of the old covenant. The shadows of temple, priest, and sacrifice now give way to the reality: Jesus himself.

The Big Picture

Jerusalem, the city that rejected the Savior, will be the first to face God's judgment. The destruction of Jerusalem signals the end of the old covenant. It also provides warning that God's final judgment is coming on all people everywhere at the end of the age.

Reflection and Discussion

Read through the complete passage for this study, Matthew 24:1–2, 15–28. Then think through and write your own notes on the following questions. (For further background see the *ESV Study Bible*, pages 1873–1874, or visit esv.org.)

As Jesus leaves the temple with his disciples, they point out to him the magnificent buildings (Matt. 24:1). More than an architectural wonder, however, the temple under the old covenant also held deep theological significance. Read 1 Kings 8:9–10, 27–30 and Psalms 46:4–7; 48:1–14. Why was the temple so important to Jesus' Jewish contemporaries?

In Matthew 24:2 Jesus prophesies that the temple will be destroyed: "There will not be left here one stone upon another." In AD 70 Roman armies laid siege to the city of Jerusalem, and on the ninth day of the Jewish month of Av (around August), Roman soldiers captured and burned the temple. Jesus' prophecy was thus clearly fulfilled within a generation. How does this help us trust the rest of Jesus' words on the Mount of Olives?

In Matthew 24:15 Jesus begins a new section of his speech by referring to the "abomination of desolation spoken of by the prophet Daniel" (see Dan. 8:13; 9:27; 11:31; 12:11). Since he encourages us to understand what we read (Matt. 24:15), turn back in your Bible to these texts in Daniel and read each of them in its context. What do they have in common? How do they help us understand what Jesus is talking about in Matthew?

Luke 21 interprets Jesus' enigmatic phrase for readers who may not be familiar with the prophecy in Daniel. How does Luke 21:20–24 confirm and clarify your understanding of what Jesus means when he speaks of the "abomination of desolation"?

In Matthew 24:21 Jesus speaks of the destruction of Jerusalem as a "great tribulation, such as has not been from the beginning of the world until now, no, and will never be." While the destruction of Jerusalem involved horrendous atrocities, subsequent Jewish history tragically includes many other calamities, including the Holocaust. Some readers therefore object that the "great tribulation" cannot refer to the destruction of Jerusalem in AD 70. But how does it help us to understand what Jesus means when we remember the significance of the temple in God's purposes (see question on Matt. 24:1 above)?

Matthew notes, when Jesus died on the cross, that the "curtain of the temple was torn in two, from top to bottom" (27:51), and Hebrews 10:19–25 provides commentary on this event. What is the theological significance of the destruction of the temple?

In Matthew 24:22 Jesus says, "If those days had not been cut short, no human being would be saved. But for the sake of the elect[1] those days will be cut short." Who are the elect? (See also 24:24, 31.) How did God's cutting short of the days of Jerusalem's destruction ensure the elect's salvation?

In Matthew 24:22–28 Jesus speaks of "false christs and false prophets," who will lead people away from Christ. How does Jesus' teaching in Matthew 7:15–23 help us to identify such false prophets even today so that we are not led away by them?

The destruction of Jerusalem serves as a warning that God's judgment will come on all who reject Jesus as their Lord and Savior. Fill in the following table to show how Jesus' teaching elsewhere in Matthew helps us to trust in Christ alone for our salvation.

Jesus' Teaching	How It Helps Us to Trust in Him
Matt. 5:1–12	
Matt. 7:24–27	
Matt. 11:25–30	
Matt. 26:26–29	

Read through the following three sections on *Gospel Glimpses*, *Whole-Bible Connections*, and *Theological Soundings*. Then take time to consider the *Personal Implications* these sections have for you.

Gospel Glimpses

THE LIGHTNING-LIKE COMING OF CHRIST. Though some people have feared that Christ has secretly returned and taken his people, leaving the rest of us behind, Jesus assures us that his return will be clear: "As the lightning comes from the east and shines as far as the west, so will be the coming of the Son of Man" (Matt. 24:27). In the Old Testament, when the Lord God comes to judge his enemies and save his people, his appearance is often associated with lightning (e.g., Ex. 19:16; Ps. 18:14; Zech. 9:14). Jesus now applies that image to his own return, showing that, in the end, he will embody the final coming of God to judge and to save his people. This will not occur in secret or be experienced only by some but will be a public, universally visible event, as unmistakable as "lightning." The Bible knows nothing of a secret return of Christ. When Jesus comes again, no one will miss it.

Whole-Bible Connections

ABOMINATION OF DESOLATION. Jesus draws his reference to the "abomination of desolation" (Matt. 24:15) from the prophet Daniel, who invariably links the abomination to the desolation of the Jerusalem temple (Dan. 8:13; 9:27; 11:31; 12:11). The phrase itself indicates something abhorrent, disgusting, and polluting that defiles the holy place ("abomination") and leads to the temple's destruction ("of desolation"). In 167 BC, when the Syrian king Antiochus Epiphanes IV desecrated the temple by offering pagan sacrifice on the altar, some Jews interpreted this as a fulfillment of Daniel's prophecy (*1 Macc.* 1:54). In Matthew 24:15, however, Jesus clearly indicates that the ultimate fulfillment was yet to come. Whether he refers to the faithlessness of Jews within the city, or the actions of the Roman army, or both, Jesus' words point to an action or set of actions that would desecrate the temple and so signal that the time had come for God's judgment upon it.

Theological Soundings

THE GREAT TRIBULATION AND THE NEW COVENANT. Jesus affirms that the "great tribulation" of AD 70 was "such as has not been from the beginning of the world until now . . . and will never be" (Matt. 24:21). This does not necessarily mean that the siege of Jerusalem involved the greatest loss of human life ever recorded or the most horrendous physical suffering ever faced. It underlines, rather, the profound significance of God's judgment on his faithless people, focused on the city that rejected his Son (Matt. 21:33–44; 22:1–7; 23:37–39). In addition the "great tribulation" of AD 70 marked the end of the old covenant—the period in which God administered his grace through the human priests, animal sacrifices, and physical tabernacle/temple that he gave to Moses at Mount Sinai. Now that Christ has come and sealed God's gracious covenant with his own blood (Matt. 26:28; cf. 1 Cor. 11:25), these shadows have been fulfilled by the realities to which they pointed (Col. 2:17; Heb. 10:1). The Lord Jesus, our great high priest, has offered the one perfect sacrifice for our sins (Heb. 4:14; 10:11–14) and opened the way for us to enter God's presence in the heavenly temple (Heb. 8:1–2; 10:19–25).

Personal Implications

Take time to reflect on the implications of Matthew 24:1–2, 15–28 for your own life today. Consider what you have learned that might lead you to praise God, repent of sin, and trust in his gracious promises. Make notes below on the personal implications for your walk with the Lord of the (1) *Gospel Glimpses*, (2) *Whole-Bible Connections*, (3) *Theological Soundings*, and (4) the passage as a whole.

1. Gospel Glimpses

2. Whole-Bible Connections

3. Theological Soundings

4. Matthew 24:1–2, 15–28

As You Finish This Unit . . .

Take a moment now to ask for the Lord's blessing and help as you continue in this study of Jesus' speech on the Mount of Olives. As you reflect on Jesus' promises for the future and what they mean for the present, pray especially that the "God of hope" might "fill you with all joy and peace in believing, so that by the power of the Holy Spirit you may abound in hope" (Rom. 15:13).

Definitions

[1] **The Elect** – Those whom God has chosen to save. Jesus refers to the "elect" three times in our passage (Matt. 24:22, 24, 31) as those in whom God shows a special interest. He cuts short the great tribulation for their sake (24:22), preserves them from being led astray by false teachers (24:24), and gathers them to himself at the end (24:31).

WEEK 4: THE COMING OF THE SON OF MAN

FINAL JUDGMENT AND SALVATION

Matthew 24:29–36

The Place of the Passage

Matthew 24:29–36 is the climax of Jesus' speech on the Mount of Olives. This short section provides the ultimate answer to the disciples' question (24:3) and draws together Jesus' promises to return, which are spread across the Gospel. In his parables about the kingdom Jesus speaks of a day when the "Son of Man"[1] will "send his angels" to gather the wicked for judgment and the righteous for eternal life (13:36–43). Following Peter's confession at Caesarea Philippi, Jesus declares that "the Son of Man is going to come with his angels in the glory of his Father" to "repay each person according to what he has done" (16:27). In his response to the high priest Jesus again announces that the Son of Man will soon be "seated at the right hand of Power" and ultimately come "on the clouds of heaven" (26:64). In each of these texts Jesus draws on the prophecy of Daniel 7:13–14 to speak of his own return from heaven in glory to execute the final judgment and usher in the fullness of God's final kingdom.

The Big Picture

At the climax of his speech Jesus announces that he will come again from heaven as the glorious "Son of Man." When he comes, Jesus will gather his people to himself and execute the final judgment on all the nations.

Reflection and Discussion

Read through the complete passage for this study, Matthew 24:29–36. Then think through and write your own notes on the following questions. (For further background see the *ESV Study Bible*, pages 1874–1875, or visit esv.org.)

Jesus now speaks of the climactic events that will occur "immediately after the tribulation of those days" (Matt. 24:29). He looks ahead, beyond the "great tribulation" of AD 70 (24:15–21) and all the troubles and persecutions of the present age (24:4–14, 22–28; cf. Rev. 7:14), to the celestial upheaval that will accompany his return. Since Jesus here employs language from several Old Testament prophecies, look at the following passages and note who comes or acts in judgment, as well as the results of his coming.

	Who comes?	What are the results of his coming?
Isa. 13:9–13		
Isa. 34:1–4		
Joel 3:14–16		
Hag. 2:6–7		
Ezek. 32:1–8		

Jesus' description of disturbances in the sun, moon, and stars (Matt. 24:29) have been interpreted literally (as a description of actual celestial upheaval) or metaphorically (as symbols for political judgment on nations and governments). What arguments could be offered for each of these interpretations?

How might Exodus 10:21–23; Joshua 10:12–14; and Matthew 27:45 shed light on this question?

In Matthew 24:30 Jesus combines the prophecies of God's coming (Matt. 24:29) with the vision of Daniel 7:13 to declare that he—the "Son of Man"—will ultimately "come" from heaven "with power and great glory." Read Daniel 7:9–14 and consider the following questions: (1) *Who* is the "son of man"—a merely human figure, or also divine? (2) *When* will he come—in the middle of history, or at the end? (3) *Where* does he end his journey—in heaven, or on earth?

In Matthew 24:30 Jesus further combines the prophecy of Daniel 7:13 with Zechariah 12:10 when he says that "all the tribes of the earth will mourn." How can we make sure that we are not among those who "mourn" on that day? What can we do to warn our family and friends?

In Matthew 24:31 Jesus turns to the joy of the final day. What is the purpose of the "loud trumpet call" (compare Ex. 19:16–17; Isa. 27:12–13; Zech. 9:14–17; 1 Cor. 15:50–57; 1 Thess. 4:13–18)? How is this good news for God's people?

In Matthew 24:32–36 Jesus relates God's judgment on Jerusalem to the final judgment at the "coming" of "the Son of Man." What are "all these things" that will occur within a generation (compare 24:34 with 24:1–3)? What are "that day and hour" about which "no one knows" (compare 24:36 with 24:27, 29–31)? How then can we "learn the lesson" of the fig tree?

In Matthew 24:33 Jesus affirms, "When you see all these things, you know that he is near, at the very gates." Paul and James repeat this affirmation in Philippians 4:4–7 and James 5:7–11. How do those passages teach us to live in light of the truth that the Lord is near?

Jesus' statement in Matthew 24:35 is breathtaking: He claims that his words, like God's words, "will not pass away" (compare Isa. 40:8). How does this statement help us to hold on to Jesus' promise to return even when life is difficult and the world seems to be descending into chaos? If it is true that Jesus' words will never pass away, what should we *do* with his words?

Read through the following three sections on *Gospel Glimpses*, *Whole-Bible Connections*, and *Theological Soundings*. Then take time to consider the *Personal Implications* these sections have for you.

Gospel Glimpses

THE LORD JESUS WILL RETURN. The *center* of the gospel is that God sent his Son, our Lord Jesus Christ, to die for the sins of his people, and to rise from the dead to give us eternal life (1 Cor. 15:3–5). Through faith in Christ, we receive now, already, God's forgiveness of our sins (e.g., Matt. 1:21), God's welcome into his family (12:50), and God's presence in our lives by the Holy Spirit (28:20). But the *climax* of the gospel is Jesus' return in glory at the end of the age (10:23; 16:27; 24:30–31; 26:64). It is only then that we will receive the fullness of God's grace to us in Christ, when he will "gather his elect" (24:31) and welcome us into "the kingdom prepared . . . from the foundation of the world" (25:34).

THE LORD WILL GATHER HIS PEOPLE. Throughout church history God's people have been scattered: by persecution (Acts 8:1), by obedience to the Great Commission (Matt. 28:18–20), and simply by the demands of life. For these and other reasons brothers and sisters in Christ, who belong together, are often separated by great distances, and ultimately by death. But Jesus offers us wonderful comfort. When he returns, "he will send out his angels" to "gather his elect" (Matt. 24:31). Then all of God's people—from every tribe and language and people and nation—will be gathered around his throne to spend eternity in his presence (Rev. 7:9–10). His gathering angels will not fail in their mission, for "the Lord knows those who are his" (2 Tim. 2:19), and not one of those who belong to the Lord will be missing. The dead will be raised, the living will be transformed (1 Cor. 15:50–52), and "we will always be with the Lord" (1 Thess. 4:17).

Whole-Bible Connections

THE SON OF MAN COMING ON THE CLOUDS. In Matthew 24:30–31 Jesus describes his return as the "coming" of the "Son of Man" using language from Daniel 7:13–14. This son of man is a human figure, a final Adam; like the first Adam, he exercises "dominion" on "earth" over the "beasts" (Dan. 7:3, 5, 6–7, 11–12, 14, 17). But he also "comes with the clouds," as only God does, exercises universal and eternal "dominion," as only God can, and receives universal worship, as only God should (Dan. 7:13–14). Jesus declares that he is that "Son of Man," who will embody the final coming of God when he descends from heaven to gather his elect and rule over all the earth. There is a sense in which Daniel's vision has begun to be fulfilled, for the Son of Man already "came not to be served but to serve" (Matt. 20:28) and has already received "all authority in heaven and on earth" (28:18). Still, Daniel's vision will reach its final fulfillment only in the future, when the Son of Man will come *again* "on the clouds of heaven with power and great glory" (24:30; cf. 16:27; 24:31, 37, 39; 26:64).

THE LAST TRUMPET TO GATHER THE ELECT. Jesus' promise in Matthew 24:30–31 combines several biblical promises regarding the end. The "trumpet" recalls the Lord's descent on Sinai (Ex. 19:16–17), the trumpets used for gathering Israel (Num. 10:1–10), and Zechariah's prophecy that "the Lord God" himself "will sound the trumpet" when he comes to save (Zech. 9:14–17). The gathering of the elect further recalls the Lord's promise that, after the exile, he will "gather" his people (e.g., Deut. 30:3–4; Isa. 40:11). Isaiah combines these elements, announcing that on the "day" when God comes to save, a "great trumpet" will call all of God's people, including those who have died, to "come and worship the Lord" (Isa. 25:6–8; 26:19–21; 27:12–13). Jesus remarkably places himself at the center of this picture: on the final day, *he* will come *as God*, with a "loud trumpet call," to "gather" his people to himself (cf. 1 Cor. 15:50–57; 1 Thess. 4:13–18).

Theological Soundings

THE LORD IS NEAR. Jesus' promise that the Lord "is near" (Matt. 24:33) has both temporal and relational dimensions. Fundamentally, God's judgment on Jerusalem in AD 70 is the sign that Jesus' final coming "is near" in a temporal sense (24:33). Although for the Lord "one day is as a thousand years, and a thousand years as one day" (2 Pet. 3:8), our final "salvation is nearer to us now than when we first believed. The night is far gone; the day is at hand" (Rom. 13:11–12). Jesus' return is the next major event on God's calendar. It will be "soon" (Rev. 22:20)! As we wait, it is a great comfort to know that the Lord is also relationally near. "The Lord is near to the brokenhearted" (Ps. 34:18) and "near to all who call on him" (Ps. 145:18). Relying on these promises, made surer by the promise of our Lord and Savior, we can with Paul "rejoice in the Lord always. . . . *The Lord is at hand*" (Phil. 4:4–5) and with James "be patient" in all our difficulties, "for *the coming of the Lord is at hand*" (James 5:8).

Personal Implications

Take time to reflect on the implications of Matthew 24:29–36 for your own life today. Consider what you have learned that might lead you to praise God, repent of sin, and trust in his gracious promises. Make notes below on the personal implications for your walk with the Lord of the (1) *Gospel Glimpses*, (2) *Whole-Bible Connections*, (3) *Theological Soundings*, and (4) the passage as a whole.

1. Gospel Glimpses

2. Whole-Bible Connections

3. Theological Soundings

4. Matthew 24:29–36

As You Finish This Unit . . .

Take a moment now to ask for the Lord's blessing and help as you continue in this study of Jesus' speech on the Mount of Olives. As you reflect on Jesus' promises for the future and what they mean for the present, pray especially that the "God of hope" might "fill you with all joy and peace in believing, so that by the power of the Holy Spirit you may abound in hope" (Rom. 15:13).

Definitions

[1] **Son of Man** – The title Jesus uses more than any other to refer to himself. Though Jesus' self-identification as "the Son of Man" may underscore his humanity (e.g., Matt. 8:20; 11:19), it especially evokes the figure in Daniel 7 who "comes on the clouds of heaven" to receive supreme authority and an everlasting kingdom over the earth (compare Dan. 7:13–14 and Matt. 24:30; 26:64).

Week 5: The Day and Hour Are Unknown

Matthew 24:36–44

The Place of the Passage

The first part of Jesus' speech on the Mount of Olives (Matt. 24:4–35) has been set against two horizons: the judgment coming on Jerusalem within a generation (esp. 24:15–21) and the judgment on all nations at the end (esp. 24:29–31). From Matthew 24:36 onward Jesus focuses on the second of these two horizons and on the need for his disciples to be ready for his return on the great final day. Jesus' earlier parables have already emphasized the judgment that will come at the "end of the age" (13:24–30, 36–43). His earlier prophecies likewise warn that on the final day the Son of Man will "come" in the "glory of his Father" to "repay each person according to what he has done" (16:27; cf. 7:21–23). Jesus now draws these threads together and emphasizes the need for faithful disciples always to be ready for his return.

The Big Picture

"No one knows" the time of the great final day when the Son of Man will come in glory to judge and to save (Matt. 24:29–36). Faithful disciples must always be ready therefore for Jesus' return.

Reflection and Discussion

Read through the complete passage for this study, Matthew 24:36–44. Then think through and write your own notes on the following questions. (For further background see the *ESV Study Bible*, pages 1875, or visit esv.org.)

Jesus now speaks of the climactic "day and hour" when he—the "Son of Man"—will come for the final judgment (Matt. 24:36). He draws on the prophets, who regularly speak of "that day" when God will come to judge his enemies and save his people. Look up the following passages and note the images they use to describe the "day of the Lord" as a day of both judgment and salvation.

	Images of Judgment	Images of Salvation
Isa. 2:10–22		
Joel 2:28–32		
Joel 3:14–21		
Zeph. 1:14–18		
Zech. 14:1–9		

In Matthew 24:36 Jesus plainly affirms that "no one knows" the "day and hour" of his return. What traps might we fall into if we forget that God has not revealed the day of Jesus' return? Why might God have chosen not to reveal to us the timing of the final judgment?

Jesus professes that even he—the incarnate Son—does not know the timing of the final day (Matt. 24:36). How might Hebrews 2:14–18 help us to understand *why* God the Son, in taking human flesh, voluntarily submitted to this human ignorance regarding the future? Do you think Jesus *now*, as the risen and exalted Son, knows when he will return?

In Matthew 24:37–39 Jesus draws a parallel between the plural "days" leading up to the singular "day" when God sent the flood at the time of Noah (Gen. 6:11–22) and the plural "days" leading up to the singular "day" when the Son of Man will come. How does this parallel provide a warning for us as we live in the days before Jesus' return?

In Matthew 24:40–42 Jesus presents two scenarios of people who are "taken" and "left" when the Son of Man comes. Those "taken" could be unbelievers who are "swept away" in the judgment (24:39) or believers who are "gathered" for salvation (24:31). Either way, Jesus draws this conclusion: "Therefore, stay awake, for you do not know on what day your Lord is coming" (24:42). What does Jesus mean by his command to "stay awake"? How is it possible to be physically awake yet spiritually "asleep"? How can we help each other to stay awake in this sense?

The apostles Paul and Peter both use Jesus' image of a thief (24:43–44) in their own teaching about Jesus' return. Read 1 Thessalonians 5:1–11 and 2 Peter 3:8–14.

Since the "day of the Lord will come like a thief" (1 Thess. 5:2; 2 Pet. 3:10), how then should we live?

At the beginning of this section of his speech Jesus says that "no one knows" the timing of "that day and hour" (Matt. 24:36). At the end of this section he draws a conclusion: "Therefore you also must be ready, for the Son of Man is coming at an hour you do not expect" (24:44). What might it look like to be unprepared for Jesus' return? How can we make sure that we are ready to meet him?

Read through the following three sections on *Gospel Glimpses*, *Whole-Bible Connections*, and *Theological Soundings*. Then take time to consider the *Personal Implications* these sections have for you.

Gospel Glimpses

GOD'S GRACE IN NOT REVEALING THE DAY. It may seem counterintuitive to say that God has been gracious to us in *not* revealing the "day and hour" of Jesus' return. But, if God made the date of the judgment known, this would only encourage sin. Fallen human beings would calculate how much sin they could get away with before the day. They would put off repentance until the last minute, and chaos would ensue. By revealing that judgment is coming, God urges us to repent of sin and to live for him. By not revealing the day, he urges us to repent now and to always be ready for our Lord's return. The Westminster Confession of Faith puts it well: "As Christ would have us to be certainly persuaded that there shall be a day of judgment, both to deter all men from sin; and for the greater consolation of the godly in their adversity: so will He have that day unknown to men, that they may shake off all carnal security, and be always watchful, because they know not at what hour the Lord will come; and may be ever prepared to say, Come Lord Jesus, come quickly, Amen" (WCF 33.3).

Whole-Bible Connections

THE FLOOD AS A TYPE OF THE FINAL JUDGMENT. Jesus appeals to the flood at the time of Noah as a type of the final judgment (Matt. 24:37–39; cf. Luke 17:26–27). The apostle Peter—following Jesus' lead—does the same (2 Pet. 2:5; 3:5–7). These texts together teach us three lessons about the final judgment. First, just as God sent the flood to destroy all life on earth for its wickedness (Gen. 6:5–7, 11–13, 17), so at the end God will judge all life on earth for the "destruction of the ungodly" (2 Pet. 3:7). Second, just as in the "days of Noah" (Matt. 24:37; Gen. 9:29) people were "unaware until the flood came and swept them all away," so the final judgment will take many by surprise (Matt. 24:38–39; cf. 2 Pet. 3:10). Third, and wonderfully, just as God preserved Noah and those with him in the ark from the flood (Gen. 6:17–22; 2 Pet. 2:5), so God will preserve all those who trust in Jesus at the final judgment (Matt. 24:31; 2 Pet. 2:9).

SIGNS AND SUDDENNESS. The disciples' question about the "sign" of Jesus' return (Matt. 24:3) has been repeated by many who want to predict the date of the end. But Jesus gives no such sign, and he warns that only the wicked ask for one (12:39; 16:4). The disturbances in sun, moon, and stars are responses to the coming of God (Matt. 24:29 with Isa. 13:9–13; 34:1–4; Joel 3:14–16; Hag. 2:6–7). The "sign of the Son of Man" is the Lord's "battle sign," raised as he comes to judge his enemies and gather his people (Matt. 24:30 with Isa. 11:12; cf. Isa. 5:26; 18:3; 49:22). These signs, therefore, provide no forewarning of the Lord's return but are part of the return itself. Certainly Jesus does lay out a series of events which must occur before the end: Jerusalem will be destroyed (Matt. 24:2, 15–22); the gospel will go to the nations (24:14); God's people will face difficulties and deceptions (24:4–14, 23–28). But "no one knows" the "day or the hour" of Jesus' return, and none of these events allows us to predict it. His coming will rather be sudden and unexpected, and we must therefore always be ready (24:36–44).

Theological Soundings

TRULY GOD AND TRULY MAN. The heretic Arius (4th century AD) reasoned from Jesus' ignorance about the final day (Matt. 24:36) to conclude that he is less than truly divine. In the Gospel of Matthew, however, Jesus is truly God and truly man. He is "God with us" (1:23; 18:20; 28:20), the "Lord" and "King" of the final judgment (7:21–23; 25:31–34), and the authoritative "Son" who shares in the singular divine "name" (28:18–19). At the same time, he is tempted and hungry (4:1–11), sleeps on a boat (8:24), and suffers and dies (27:32–54). The church therefore confesses, in the words of the Creed of Chalcedon (AD 451), that "our Lord Jesus Christ" is "truly God and truly man"; in his "one person," the "two natures" of God and man are not "confused," "changed," "divided," or "separated" but perfectly united. For this reason orthodox readers have rightly understood that in Matthew 24:36 Jesus speaks of his ignorance according to his human nature. As God, he knows all things (e.g., Ps. 147:5; Isa. 46:10; Heb. 4:13). As man, he does not. While we cannot understand the depths of this mystery, we rightly stand in awe and wonder: the eternal Son of God took human nature *for us and our salvation*.

Personal Implications

Take time to reflect on the implications of Matthew 24:36–44 for your own life today. Consider what you have learned that might lead you to praise God, repent of sin, and trust in his gracious promises. Make notes below on the personal implications for your walk with the Lord of the (1) *Gospel Glimpses*, (2) *Whole-Bible Connections*, (3) *Theological Soundings*, and (4) the passage as a whole.

1. Gospel Glimpses

2. Whole-Bible Connections

3. Theological Soundings

4. Matthew 24:36–44

As You Finish This Unit . . .

Take a moment now to ask for the Lord's blessing and help as you continue in this study of Jesus' speech on the Mount of Olives. As you reflect on Jesus' promises for the future and what they mean for the present, pray especially that the "God of hope" might "fill you with all joy and peace in believing, so that by the power of the Holy Spirit you may abound in hope" (Rom. 15:13).

WEEK 6: PREPARE FOR HIS RETURN

WISE AND WICKED SERVANTS

Matthew 24:45–51

The Place of the Passage

In Matthew 24:45–51 Jesus moves from teaching about his return to teaching about how faithful disciples ought to live while they wait for that return. Jesus signals this transition by his rhetorical question in verse 45: "Who then is the faithful and wise servant?" Jesus' representation of himself as a "Lord" or "master" with "servants" or "slaves" picks up on his use of the same image in other parables earlier in the Gospel (13:24–30; 18:23–35; 21:33–44; 22:1–14). He continues to use this image in the parables that follow (25:1–46). It emphasizes Jesus' lordship over his disciples, and it reminds us that ultimately we are accountable to him for how we live as we wait for his return.

The Big Picture

Jesus urges his disciples to prepare for his return by faithfully discharging the duties he has entrusted to us, especially the duty to care for fellow disciples.

Reflection and Discussion

Read through the complete passage for this study, Matthew 24:45–51. Then think through and write your own notes on the following questions. (For further background see the *ESV Study Bible*, page 1875, or visit esv.org.)

Jesus first addresses the "faithful and wise servant, whom his master has set over his household" (Matt. 24:45). While this parable applies generally to all Christians, it applies most directly to those "set over" God's "household"—first the twelve apostles, then the elders and deacons whom the Lord has set over his church. Within the parable the master charges his servants to give their fellow servants "food at the proper time." How do the passages in the table below fill out the primary responsibilities of those whom the Lord has "set over" his church?

	Type of Servant	Primary Responsibilities
Acts 20:17, 28		
Eph. 4:11–12		
1 Tim. 3:1–7; 5:17		
Titus 1:5–9		
1 Pet. 5:1–4		
Acts 6:1–7		
1 Tim. 3:8–13		

In Matthew 24:45–47 Jesus promises reward to the "faithful and wise servant" whom the "master" finds discharging his duties "when he comes." This servant is "blessed," and the master will "set him over all his possessions." How should this promise of reward motivate us to serve the Lord faithfully in the duties he has assigned to each of us?

In Matthew 24:48–49 Jesus contrasts the "faithful and wise servant" with a "wicked servant." What does this servant's behavior reveal about his attitude toward the master and his fellow servants? How is his behavior fueled by his lack of faith?

The wicked servant's lack of faith is focused particularly on Jesus' promise to return. He "says to himself, 'my master is delayed'" (Matt. 24:48). Following Jesus' lead, both Paul and Peter warn of the spiritual danger of downplaying or denying Jesus' return. How do 1 Thessalonians 5:1–11 and 2 Peter 3:1–7 amplify and apply Jesus' warnings?

Jesus warns that the "wicked servant" will be placed with the "hypocrites" (Matt. 24:50–51). Jesus refers to hypocrisy[1] elsewhere to speak of those who wear a mask of godliness but only play at faith in God. Look up the following references to "hypocrites" and make a list of their characteristics: Matthew 6:2, 5, 16; 7:1–5: 15:3–9; 22:15–22; 23:13–15, 23, 25, 27, 29–31. What is the difference between a faithful disciple struggling with sin and a hypocrite?

Jesus describes the final state of the "wicked servant" in striking terms: "the master . . . will cut him in pieces and put him with the hypocrites. In that place there will be weeping and gnashing of teeth" (24:50–51; cf. 8:12; 13:42, 50; 22:13; 25:30). Although this description appears in a parable, it is certainly designed to help us feel the weight of facing God's righteous judgment. How should a "faithful and wise servant" respond to the knowledge that judgment is coming on the wicked?

Jesus places himself at the center of the judgment scene. It is "*the master*" who "will cut [the wicked servant] in pieces and put him with the hypocrites" (24:50–51). Why is it important to recognize that Jesus himself will personally execute the final judgment?

Look back over the parable we have studied (24:45–51). How would you summarize the difference between a "wise and faithful servant" and a "wicked servant"? How can we encourage each other to continue as "wise and faithful servants" until the master returns?

Read through the following three sections on *Gospel Glimpses*, *Whole-Bible Connections*, and *Theological Soundings*. Then take time to consider the *Personal Implications* these sections have for you.

Gospel Glimpses

THE JUDGE FACED THE JUDGMENT IN OUR PLACE. Jesus' parable of the wise and wicked servant warns us of the reality that our Lord will come to judge and encourages us to serve him faithfully until he returns (24:45–51). But Jesus' parable should also remind us that the Judge has faced the judgment in our place. On the road to Jerusalem Jesus declared, "The Son of Man came . . . to give his life as a ransom for many" (20:28). At the Last Supper he explained that his blood would be "poured out for many for the forgiveness of sins" (26:28). In the garden of Gethsemane he willingly accepted that he should drink the "cup" of God's wrath (26:36–46). Finally, on the cross, as he cried out, "My God, my God, why have you forsaken me?" (27:46), he showed that in his death he bore God's righteous judgment against sin. The Judge of the final day suffered willingly the judgment in our place. He bore the punishment in place of the "many" so that any who repents and believes the gospel will find forgiveness and life in him.

Whole-Bible Connections

THE DANGER OF DENYING THE LORD'S RETURN. The "wicked servant" in Jesus' parable downplays his Lord's return when he says to himself, "My master is delayed" (24:48). It is this faithless thought that leads to his wicked behavior (24:49). Paul and Peter both similarly warn that faithless people will downplay or even deny the Lord's return to excuse their wicked behavior. Paul warns, "While people are saying, 'There is peace and security,' then sudden destruction will come upon them" (1 Thess. 5:3). Like Jesus, he links this attitude to sleep and drunkenness (1 Thess. 5:7 with Matt. 24:43, 49; 25:5). By contrast Christian believers, who belong to "the day" and "the light," are to live in faith, love, and hope in Jesus' return (1 Thess. 5:4–9). Peter similarly warns that "scoffers" will deny the Lord's return (2 Pet. 3:3–4), but he encourages believers to live in "holiness and godliness" as we wait for the great final day (2 Pet. 3:11).

Theological Soundings

REWARDS AT THE JUDGMENT. In our parable (Matt. 24:46–47), as elsewhere in Matthew, Jesus promises that faithful disciples will be rewarded at the judgment (6:4, 6, 18–20; 10:40–42; 19:29; 25:21, 23, 34). Just as the reward for practicing piano is the joy of playing music, so the reward for faithfully serving the Lord is to continue serving him in an even greater capacity (24:47; 25:21, 23). Since we owe everything we have and everything we are to God, the

Lord's rewards are not payments for services rendered but gifts of his grace (cf. Luke 17:10). The faithful servant is faithful only because the Lord has made him so. This is why Jesus also says that faithful disciples will "inherit" eternal life in the kingdom of God (Matt. 19:29; 25:34). Our reward is not a payment we merit but a gift we inherit from our loving heavenly Father. When all is said and done, the Lord himself is our reward, for on the final day he will say to those who have faithfully served him: "Well done, good and faithful servant. . . . *Enter into the joy of your master*" (25:21, 23).

Personal Implications

Take time to reflect on the implications of Matthew 24:45–51 for your own life today. Consider what you have learned that might lead you to praise God, repent of sin, and trust in his gracious promises. Make notes below on the personal implications for your walk with the Lord of the (1) *Gospel Glimpses*, (2) *Whole-Bible Connections*, (3) *Theological Soundings*, and (4) the passage as a whole.

1. Gospel Glimpses

2. Whole-Bible Connections

3. Theological Soundings

4. Matthew 24:45–51

As You Finish This Unit . . .

Take a moment now to ask for the Lord's blessing and help as you continue in this study of Jesus' speech on the Mount of Olives. As you reflect on Jesus' promises for the future and what they mean for the present, pray, especially, that the "God of hope" might "fill you with all joy and peace in believing, so that by the power of the Holy Spirit you may abound in hope" (Rom. 15:13).

Definitions

[1] **Hypocrisy** – Falsely presenting oneself to others in order to gain positive regard or praise. Derived from Greek for "actor." Jesus repeatedly condemned the hypocrisy of the religious leaders of his day.

Week 7: Be Always Ready

Wise and Foolish Virgins

Matthew 25:1–13

The Place of the Passage

Jesus' parable of the virgins is unique to the Gospel of Matthew and amplifies the notes of both joy and warning that Jesus has sounded earlier in the Gospel. On the one hand, although Jesus earlier warned that "the bridegroom" would one day be "taken away" from the "wedding guests" (9:14–17), he now adds that "the bridegroom" will ultimately return to welcome those ready for him into the joy of the marriage feast (25:10). Their joy will be full! On the other hand, just as Jesus earlier warned that on the final day he would not recognize some who called him "Lord, Lord," so he now confirms that some who appear to be waiting for him will miss out on the marriage feast (7:21–23; 25:11–12). In these two elements of his parable Jesus amplifies the joy of the final day and the horror of being unprepared, thus urging us always to be ready for his return.

The Big Picture

Jesus' parable of the virgins contrasts the wisdom of those who are ready for the Lord's return with the folly of those who are not, thus encouraging us always to be ready to welcome the Lord when he comes.

Reflection and Discussion

Read through the complete passage for this study, Matthew 25:1–13. Then think through and write your own notes on the following questions. (For further background see the *ESV Study Bible*, page 1876, or visit esv.org.)

Jesus introduces his parable of the virgins with the statement "*Then* the kingdom of heaven[1] *will be* like" (Matt. 25:1). Compared to similar phrases earlier in the Gospel (13:24, 31, 33, 44, 45, 47; 18:23; 20:1; 22:2), what is unique about Jesus' introduction to this parable? How does this unique introduction clarify the focus and intent of the parable?

In Jesus' prophecies about his own return he has so far referred to himself as the "Son of Man" (Matt. 24:27, 30, 37, 39, 44) and the "Lord" or "master" (24:42, 50). He now adds the striking image of "the bridegroom" (25:1), which is drawn from the Old Testament prophets. Read the following verses in context and see who is the husband or bridegroom of God's people. How does this help us better understand Jesus' promise to return?

	Husband/Bridegroom
Isa. 54:5; 62:5	
Jer. 31:32	
Ezek. 16:8, 32, 45	
Hos. 2:16, 19–20	
Matt. 9:15	

In Jewish wedding customs in the first century the groom would usually leave his parents' house, accompanied by friends, to collect his bride and her bridesmaids from her parents' house before returning in procession to his own parents' house for the marriage feast. The "virgins" in Jesus' parable are the unmarried bridesmaids, who would go out to meet the bridegroom and welcome him as he comes. Read Matthew 25:2–5 again. What *similarities* and *differences* does Jesus draw between "wise" and "foolish virgins"? How does this show us what it means to be a wise disciple today?

In Matthew 25:5 Jesus explains, "As the bridegroom was delayed, they all became drowsy and slept." In Jesus' earlier parable the wicked servant uses his master's delay as an excuse for his wicked behavior (24:48–49). Similarly, Jesus and the apostles elsewhere use sleep as a metaphor for spiritual unpreparedness (24:42–43; Eph. 5:14; 1 Thess. 5:6–7). In this parable, is the sleep of the virgins necessarily a bad thing? How might someone sleep physically while remaining spiritually awake?

In Matthew 25:6, a cry goes out, announcing, "Here is the bridegroom!" and calling on the virgins to "come out to meet him." While this is a natural feature of Jesus' story, the description of a cry or loud voice that calls God's people to meet him as he comes has deep roots in the Old Testament and also appears in related New Testament passages. Read Exodus 19:16–20; Joel 3:14–21; John 5:25, 28–29; and 1 Thessalonians 4:16–17. How do these passages help us to imagine that great day?

In Matthew 25:7–9 the foolish virgins ask the wise for some of their oil, but the wise refuse. Earlier in the Gospel Jesus commanded his disciples, “Give to the one who begs from you, and do not refuse the one who would borrow from you” (5:42). Are the wise virgins being disobedient and unkind? Are they wise in this instance to withhold oil?

The end of the parable comes as a shock. The foolish virgins are not “ready” when the bridegroom comes and are shut out of the marriage feast. Although they think they know the bridegroom and address him as “Lord, lord,” it turns out he does not know them (25:10–12). This shocking scene picks up a thread in Matthew’s Gospel in which people who think they are “in” ultimately find themselves “out” of God’s kingdom. Read the following passages and note the characteristics of those who are welcomed in and those who are shut out.

	Welcomed In	Shut Out
Matt. 7:21–23		
Matt. 8:5–13		
Matt. 13:24–30, 36–43		
Matt. 22:1–14		

While the foolish virgins are shut out, the wise virgins are welcomed into the marriage feast (Matt. 25:10). This is a common biblical image for the final kingdom of God. Read the following passages and note how they expand our vision of the joy and celebration of life in the final kingdom of God: Exodus 24:9–11; Isaiah 25:6–9; Matthew 8:10–12; and Revelation 19:6–9.

In Matthew 25:13 Jesus draws the lesson of the parable: "Watch therefore, for you know neither the day nor the hour." For what are we to "watch" (compare 24:42–43, where the same verb is translated "stay awake")? What does this "watching" involve in terms of our practical, daily lives as Christians?

Read through the following three sections on *Gospel Glimpses*, *Whole-Bible Connections*, and *Theological Soundings*. Then take time to consider the *Personal Implications* these sections have for you.

Gospel Glimpses

OUR LORD MAY SEEM DELAYED. Jesus promises that his return is "near" (24:33, 42–44, 50; 25:10, 13) but never puts a date on that final day. His promise that "some" disciples "will . . . see the Son of Man coming in his kingdom" (16:28) was fulfilled in the transfiguration, when Peter, James, and John received a preview of Jesus' future glory (17:1–8). His announcement that "this generation will not pass away until all these things take place" (24:34) was fulfilled in AD 70, when Jerusalem was destroyed (24:34 with 24:1–3). But, Jesus says, "no one knows" about "*that* day and hour"—the time of his return (24:36). In fact, Jesus indicates that there will be a significant period of waiting before he comes. His blood, he says, renews God's covenant, which in its earlier form stood for over a thousand years (26:28). The gospel, he affirms, must be "proclaimed throughout *the whole world*" before "the end" (24:14; cf. 28:18–20). The bridegroom, he warns, may be delayed (25:5), and the master will return only "after a long time" (25:19). Jesus' assurance that his return is "near," is not a chronological specification, therefore, but a theological affirmation: it is the next major event on God's calendar. We should therefore "count the patience of our Lord as salvation" since it gives us and others time to repent and be reconciled to God before the great final day (2 Pet. 3:15).

Whole-Bible Connections

JESUS OUR BRIDEGROOM. The Old Testament describes God regularly as the "husband" of his people (Isa. 54:5; Jer. 31:32; Ezek. 16:8, 32, 45; Hos. 2:16,

19–20), and once as the "bridegroom" who comes to save them (Isa. 62:4–5, 11), but never describes the promised (human) Messiah in these terms. In applying this image to himself (Matt. 25:1, 5–6, 10) Jesus promises that he will embody *God's* long-promised coming to his people. This is remarkable, for in his earlier response to John the Baptist's disciples he explained that the bridegroom first came only to be "taken away" in his death (9:15). In God's mysterious purposes this was the means by which our bridegroom washed us clean from our sins and so purified us to present us to himself "in splendor . . . holy and without blemish" (Eph. 5:25–27). What is more, in this going away our bridegroom has gone to "prepare a place" for his bride, the church, so that, when he comes again, he will draw us to himself (John 14:2–3). When our bridegroom returns, he will welcome those who are waiting for him into the joy of the wedding feast (Matt. 25:10; Rev. 19:6–9), and we will dwell with him as his bride forever (Rev. 21:2–3, 9; 22:17).

Theological Soundings

THE INVISIBLE CHURCH. Jesus' teaching in Matthew confronts us with the reality that some who address him as "Lord, Lord" do not truly belong to him (Matt. 7:21–23). Some who are outwardly "sons of the kingdom" will miss out on the feast (8:11–12). Some who grow in the same field as the "good seed" are really "weeds" (13:24–30, 36–43). Some who appear to be waiting for the bridegroom will not be ready when he comes (25:1–13). Christian theology, therefore, distinguishes between the visible and the invisible church. The visible church can be seen with our eyes. It consists of all those throughout history, and around the world, who profess faith in Christ, and is often thought to include their children as well. The invisible church, by contrast, cannot yet be seen. It consists of all God's chosen people, whom he is gathering to himself as the Spirit brings them to saving faith in Christ. This invisible church will become visible on the great final day (Rev. 7:9–10). In the meantime Jesus' teaching serves as a warning. It is possible to profess faith in Christ outwardly and to be a member, or even a leader, of the church while not truly trusting Christ for salvation. Paul therefore urges us, "Examine yourselves, to see whether you are in the faith" (2 Cor. 13:5). At the same time, since our salvation depends ultimately not on us but on God, who has mercy (Rom. 9:16), we need not be anxious. God's promises are sure, his grace deep, and thus "everyone who calls on the name of the Lord will be saved" (Rom. 10:13).

Personal Implications

Take time to reflect on the implications of Matthew 25:1–13 for your own life today. Consider what you have learned that might lead you to praise God, repent of sin,

and trust in his gracious promises. Make notes below on the personal implications for your walk with the Lord of the (1) *Gospel Glimpses*, (2) *Whole-Bible Connections*, (3) *Theological Soundings*, and (4) the passage as a whole.

1. Gospel Glimpses

2. Whole-Bible Connections

3. Theological Soundings

4. Matthew 25:1–13

As You Finish This Unit . . .

Take a moment now to ask for the Lord's blessing and help as you continue in this study of Jesus' speech on the Mount of Olives. As you reflect on Jesus' promises for the future and what they mean for the present, pray, especially, that the "God of hope" might "fill you with all joy and peace in believing, so that by the power of the Holy Spirit you may abound in hope" (Rom. 15:13).

Definitions

[1] **Kingdom of heaven** – The sovereign and saving rule of God over heaven and earth. The phrase "kingdom of heaven" is unique to Matthew in the New Testament, but it is synonymous with "kingdom of God." At the present time, the fallen, sinful world is in rebellion against God's kingdom. Instead, God's kingdom can be found in heaven and among his people (Matt. 6:9–10; Luke 17:20–21). When Christ returns as king, he will sit on his glorious throne, end all rebellion, gather his people, and establish God's final kingdom in the "new world" (16:27; 19:28; 24:30–31; 25:31).

Week 8: Invest for Eternity

Faithful and Slothful Stewards

Matthew 25:14–30

The Place of the Passage

In his parable of the talents[1] (Matt. 25:14–30) Jesus provides us with a further picture of what the "kingdom of heaven" will be like when he returns (25:14 refers to 25:1), so that we can live faithfully for him in the present. Jesus here expands his earlier brief parable about the returning master, which urges disciples to prepare for his return by discharging faithfully the duties entrusted to them (24:45–51). The earlier parable especially warns against denying or downplaying his return as an excuse for wicked behavior. In this later parable Jesus emphasizes that "watching" and "waiting" for his return entail not passive inactivity but faithful, active service to extend his kingdom.

The Big Picture

As we wait for Jesus' return, he calls us to serve him actively with the abilities, opportunities, resources, responsibilities, and relationships he has entrusted to us.

Reflection and Discussion

Read through the complete passage for this study, Matthew 25:14–30. Then think through and write your own notes on the following questions. (For further background see the *ESV Study Bible*, pages 1876–1877, or visit esv.org.)

Jesus introduces the parable by likening the "kingdom of heaven" to "a man going on a journey" who entrusts his servants with his property (25:14) and expects them to make good use of it until he returns (25:27). How does the shape of the man's journey parallel Jesus' resurrection, ascension, and future return?

Jesus' parable pictures the "master" as entrusting his "servants" with "talents" (Matt. 25:15)—large sums of money. In the early church these talents were often interpreted as a symbol for the treasure of God's Word. In modern interpretation the talents have often been taken to represent the abilities or responsibilities the Lord grants to each of us. Which of these interpretations makes better sense of the parable? Or are both equally suitable?

In Jesus' parable the master entrusts differing degrees of responsibility to each servant—"to each according to his ability" (25:15). Paul and Peter apply the same principle in their teaching regarding spiritual gifts (e.g., Rom. 12:6; 1 Cor. 12:7; Eph 4:7; 1 Pet. 4:10). How might remembering this truth help us to serve our Lord faithfully and free us from comparing ourselves to others?

Jesus pictures the master's return "after a long time" (Matt. 25:19). In the previous parable he pictured the bridegroom as "delayed" (25:5). How do we hold together this teaching, that the Lord will only return "after a long time," with Jesus' insistence that we must always "be ready," for he will come "at an hour [we] do not expect" (24:44, 50; 25:13)?

When the master returns, he settles accounts with his servants (25:19). What difference does this settling of accounts reveal between the faithful servants and the wicked servant (25:20–30)? In each case how does their attitude toward the master affect their behavior?

The wicked servant claims to know the master: "I knew you to be a hard man, reaping where you did not sow, and gathering where you scattered no seed" (25:24). Is this an accurate description of the master in the parable? Is this an accurate description of Jesus in Matthew (consider 9:36; 11:28–30; 14:14; 15:32; 20:16)? How can we avoid finding ourselves in the position of the wicked slave, thinking we know the Lord when in reality we do not?

The wicked servant is described as "slothful" and "worthless" (25:26, 30). He is stripped of his talent and cast into the outer darkness, according to the law of the kingdom (25:28–30; cf. 13:12). How does his example provide a warning for us?

The master rewards his faithful servants with greater responsibility and with entry into the master's joy (25:21, 23). How does this help us to imagine the final state of the righteous in the kingdom of heaven? How should this promise of reward motivate our service?

Spend some time reflecting on what the Lord has entrusted to you. Consider your abilities, opportunities, resources, responsibilities, and relationships. What does it mean, in practical terms, to invest what the Lord has entrusted to you in ways that will bring a return for his kingdom? Are there ways in which you are failing to steward well what he has entrusted to you and from which you should repent?

Read through the following three sections on *Gospel Glimpses*, *Whole-Bible Connections*, and *Theological Soundings*. Then take time to consider the *Personal Implications* these sections have for you.

Gospel Glimpses

REAL RESPONSIBILITY AND RICH REWARD. God does not need us to care for and sustain his world, for "the LORD has established his throne in the heavens, and his kingdom rules over all" (Ps. 103:19). Yet in his common grace he entrusts those made in his image with real responsibility to "fill," "subdue," and exercise "dominion" over the earth (Gen. 1:28). God also does not need us to build his church and extend his kingdom, for Jesus has "all authority in heaven and on earth," and *he* will build *his* church (Matt. 16:18; 28:18). Yet in his saving grace he entrusts those whom he saves with real responsibility, charging each of us to play our part in the church's mission to "make disciples of all nations" (28:19–20). What a precious privilege! What grace! And what further grace that when we do serve him faithfully, he promises us a warm welcome into his eternal kingdom, even greater responsibility in it, and—best of all—a share in his own joy (25:21, 23). Let us, then, "serve the LORD with gladness" (Ps. 100:2), for in his service there is perfect freedom.

Whole-Bible Connections

VARIED GIFTS AND INDIVIDUAL RESPONSIBILITY TO THE LORD. Jesus' parable of the talents teaches the important biblical truth that each of us is responsible to the Lord for ourselves. Just as the master in the parable entrusts different amounts of money to each servant—"to each according to his ability" (Matt. 25:15)—so the apostles teach us that the Lord gifts each believer differently: "Grace was given to each one of us according to the measure of Christ's gift" (Eph. 4:7); "To each is given the manifestation of the Spirit for the common good" (1 Cor. 12:7); we have "gifts that differ according to the grace given to us" (Rom. 12:6); therefore, "as each has received a gift, use it to serve one another, as good stewards of God's varied grace" (1 Pet. 4:10). Since it is the holy, wise, and good Lord who distributes gifts to his people, we can be confident that the gifts he gives are just, right, and good. When we recognize and rest in this truth, it frees us from being jealous of the gifts he has given to others. We can then serve him wholeheartedly and faithfully according to the gifts he has given us and in the callings he has placed on each of our lives.

Theological Soundings

JUDGMENT ACCORDING TO WORKS, BUT SALVATION ALL OF GRACE. When the Lord comes to settle accounts with his servants, the "good and faithful servant" is rewarded, while the "wicked," "slothful," "worthless" servant is condemned (Matt. 25:21, 23, 26, 28–30). This principle of judgment *according to* works is consistent with Jesus' teaching elsewhere (12:36–37; 16:27; John 5:28–29), and with Scripture as whole (Ps. 62:12; Prov. 24:12; 2 Cor. 5:10; 1 Pet. 1:17; Rev. 20:12–13). Scripture, however, nowhere teaches judgment *on the basis of* works. This may seem a fine distinction, but it is an important one. Our salvation is all of grace. It is the "gift of God, not a result of works, so that no one may boast" (Eph. 2:8–9). God saves us on the basis of what he has done—outside of us, without us, and for us—in Jesus' life, death, and resurrection (1 Cor. 15:1–4). When God saves us, however, he so unites us to Christ and fills us with his Spirit that we begin to live for him. So, while we are not saved by good works or on the basis of good works, we are saved for them

(Eph. 2:10; James 2:14–26). Our good works, however feeble and faltering, are nevertheless important evidence of the true faith he has given us. Thus, when the Lord judges us according to our works, he is judging us according to the evidence that he has saved us by his grace alone, through faith alone, in Christ alone.

Personal Implications

Take time to reflect on the implications of Matthew 25:14–30 for your own life today. Consider what you have learned that might lead you to praise God, repent of sin, and trust in his gracious promises. Make notes below on the personal implications for your walk with the Lord of the (1) *Gospel Glimpses*, (2) *Whole-Bible Connections*, (3) *Theological Soundings*, and (4) the passage as a whole.

1. Gospel Glimpses

2. Whole-Bible Connections

3. Theological Soundings

4. Matthew 25:14–30

As You Finish This Unit . . .

Take a moment now to ask for the Lord's blessing and help as you continue in this study of Jesus' speech on the Mount of Olives. As you reflect on Jesus' promises for the future and what they mean for the present, pray, especially, that the "God of hope" might "fill you with all joy and peace in believing, so that by the power of the Holy Spirit you may abound in hope" (Rom. 15:13).

Definitions

[1] **Talent** – The Greek word *talanton* appears in the New Testament only in Matthew (18:24; 25:15–28). In the Old Testament period it referred to a measure of weight equaling about 75 pounds (34 kg). In the New Testament period it was a unit of monetary reckoning (not an actual coin) valued at about 6,000 denarii. Since a common laborer earned about one denarius per day (20:2), a talent was a very large sum of money—about twenty years' wages. The English word *talent* is derived from this Greek word.

WEEK 9: LOVE THE KING'S FAMILY

SHEEP AND GOATS

Matthew 25:31–46

The Place of the Passage

Matthew 25:31–46 is not so much a parable as a prophecy in which Jesus provides his most extensive picture of his return for the final judgment. The scene is set "when the Son of Man comes in his glory," gathers "before him . . . all the nations," and places each person either on his right or on his left (as "sheep" or "goats") to receive final commendation or condemnation (25:31–33). The scene recalls Jesus' repeated affirmations that the Son of Man will "come" to execute final judgment (10:23; 13:41; 16:27; 19:28; 24:30; 26:64). It further recalls his repeated warnings of a final separation between the righteous and the wicked (7:21–23; 8:11–12; 13:41–43, 49–50; 22:10–14; 24:46–51; 25:10–12, 19–30). Crucially, it also recalls his teaching that to receive his disciples is to welcome Jesus himself (10:40–42). Now, however, Jesus paints the scene in full color as he lifts our eyes to the great final day.

The Big Picture

When the Lord Jesus comes in his glory, he will gather before his throne everyone who has ever lived, and he will welcome those who have loved him into the joy of his presence in his eternal kingdom, while casting out forever those who have rejected him.

Reflection and Discussion

Read through the complete passage for this study, Matthew 25:31–46. Then think through and write your own notes on the following questions. (For further background see the *ESV Study Bible*, page 1877, or visit esv.org.)

In Matthew 25:31–34 Jesus paints the scene of the final judgment by drawing on several Old Testament passages. Complete the table below by noting the elements of the scene drawn from each passage and what each teaches us about Jesus himself and the final day.

	Element in Matt. 25:31–34	Identity of Jesus	The Final Day
Dan. 7:13–14			
Isa. 66:18–19			
Deut. 33:2			
Ezek. 43:2–5; 44:4			
Jer. 14:21; 17:12			
Zech. 14:2, 5, 9			
Ezek. 34:17			

In Matthew 25:31–34 Jesus also draws together several elements from his own prophecies and so brings to a climax both his claims about himself and his promises for the future. Complete the table below by noting the elements of the scene drawn from each passage and what each teaches us about Jesus himself and the final day.

	Element in Matt. 25:31–34	Identity of Jesus	The Final Day
Matt. 10:23			
Matt. 13:36–43			
Matt. 16:27–28			
Matt. 19:28–30			
Matt. 24:30–31			
Matt. 26:64			

The king first addresses the "sheep" (25:34–40). On the one hand he describes these people as recipients of God's free grace (25:34; cf. 24:22, 24, 31). On the other hand he describes them in terms of the good that they have done (25:35–40). How can we best explain the relationship between these two realities?

The king emphasizes that, in caring for others, the "righteous" have cared for *him* (25:40). Although Christians are called to show concern for the welfare of all people (Gal. 6:10), Jesus here has a more specific group of people in mind. According to Matthew (Matt. 12:46–50; 23:8; 28:10) whom does Jesus identify as his "brothers"? How does these passages help to clarify the focus of Jesus' encouragement to the righteous in Matthew 25:34–40?

The king next addresses the "goats" (25:41–46). They call him "Lord" (25:44), but only because his glory has now been revealed (25:31–33). Their whole lives have demonstrated that they do not know him, and he condemns them for their failure to welcome *him*, expressed in their failure to care for "the least of these" (25:42–45). Elsewhere Jesus teaches that people who reject him will also reject his disciples (5:11–12; 10:24–25; 24:9). Where have you seen this reality in the world today? How can it help us to face pressure, persecution, or indifference when we know that the world's opposition to the Lord's people is rooted in its opposition to the Lord himself?

The king pronounces a curse upon the "goats," banishes them from his presence, and sends them into the "eternal punishment" of "eternal fire" (25:41, 46; cf. 5:22; 7:23; 18:8–9). In contrast to the "kingdom," which was prepared for the righteous (25:34), the "eternal fire," Jesus says, was prepared "for the devil[1] and his angels" (25:41). What does this difference suggest about God's heart toward the righteous and the wicked? How should it lead us to respond to those who do not yet recognize Jesus as Lord?

James and John apply Jesus' teaching in Matthew 25:31–46 to Christian believers. Read the following passages and note the commands, then consider how to apply these commands in the location and time in which the Lord has placed you: James 1:27; 2:14–17; 1 John 3:16–18; 4:7–12, 19–21.

Jesus concludes his speech on the Mount of Olives with the promise of "eternal life" in God's final "kingdom" (25:34, 46). Read Matthew 5:3–12; 6:10, 33; 8:11–12; 13:41–43; 19:28–30. How do these passages add to our understanding of what life will be like in God's final kingdom?

Read through the following three sections on *Gospel Glimpses*, *Whole-Bible Connections*, and *Theological Soundings*. Then take time to consider the *Personal Implications* these sections have for you.

Gospel Glimpses

KINGDOM AND ETERNAL LIFE. On the final day the King, Jesus himself, will welcome his people into God's final "kingdom," where there is "eternal life" (25:34, 46). In God's final kingdom "the devil and his angels" and "all causes of sin" will be cast out (7:21–23; 13:41–42; 25:41), and "every disease and every affliction" will be healed (4:23; 9:35). God's "will" shall be done "on earth as it is in heaven" (6:10), and the whole creation shall be renewed (19:28) to become a place of "righteousness" (6:33; cf. 2 Pet. 3:13). God's people will receive the fullness of God's "mercy," "comfort," and "satisfaction" and will "inherit the earth" (Matt. 5:3–8). The righteous will receive their reward (5:10–12, 44–48; 6:4, 6, 18; 10:40–42; 19:29; 25:34–40) and "shine like the sun in the kingdom of their Father" (13:43). The faithful will hear the Lord's words, "Well done, good and faithful servant," and be entrusted with greater responsibility (25:21, 23). Life in that kingdom will be like a great banquet, or wedding feast (8:11; 22:2–4, 9), with Jesus himself as the host (25:10; 26:29). And—best of all—those welcomed into God's final kingdom will know the "blessing" of their heavenly "Father" (5:3–11; 6:9; 13:43; 25:34; 26:29), will be called "sons of God" (5:9), and "shall see God" face to face (5:8).

Whole-Bible Connections

THE FINAL KINGDOM OF GOD. Jesus' promise to his people that they will "inherit the kingdom prepared . . . from before the foundation of the world" (Matt. 25:34) points to the final kingdom of God. God is, of course, king over all creation from the very beginning. Since Adam and Eve rebelled against their Creator, however, God's rule has been rejected by humans. Through his prophets in the Old Testament, therefore, God announced a future day when he could come as king to reestablish his reign over all the earth (e.g., Zech. 14:5, 9). When Jesus came, he announced that "the kingdom of heaven is at hand" (Matt. 4:17), he enacted God's kingdom in his mighty works (12:28), and he established God's kingdom through his death and resurrection (28:18). Still, God's kingdom has not yet come in all its fullness. We therefore continue to pray, as Jesus taught us, "Your kingdom come, your will be done, on earth as it is in heaven" (6:10). When Jesus returns as king, he will finally establish God's kingdom in all its fullness.

BROTHERLY LOVE. Jesus' final prophecy highlights the importance of loving those whom he calls his "brothers" (25:34–40), that is, Jesus' own disciples (10:40–42; 12:46–50; 23:8; 28:10). This teaching—that believers must show love in practical ways to fellow believers—is consistent throughout Scripture. Prior to Jesus, God commanded Israel to show love toward the poor, widows, orphans, and others in need (e.g., Lev. 19:10; 23:22; Deut. 15:7–11; 24:17–22; Prov. 14:31). After Jesus, Paul learned that to persecute Christians was to persecute the Lord himself (Acts 9:4–5). More positively, the apostles all teach us to "love one another" (Rom. 12:10; 1 Pet. 1:22; 1 John 4:7) and to show this love in practical ways (James 1:27; 2:8, 15–16; 1 John 3:18). Our love for each other is rooted in God's fatherly love for his children, demonstrated supremely in Christ (1 John 4:10–11, 19), and is an expression of the second great commandment (Lev. 19:18; Matt. 22:39; Rom. 13:9; Gal. 5:14; James 2:8). So, while God commands us to "do good to everyone," he "especially" commands us to show love "to those who are of the household of faith" (Gal. 6:10).

Theological Soundings

BEFORE THE FOUNDATION OF THE WORLD. The final "kingdom" of God was "prepared" for "the righteous" from the "foundation of the world" (Matt. 25:34). The Bible in fact clearly teaches that God, before the creation of the world, decreed all that should occur, including the salvation of his chosen people.

The Father knew and loved the Son "before the foundation of the world" (John 17:24; 1 Pet. 1:20). God knows the end from the beginning because he decreed it in advance (Isa. 46:8–11). All our days were written in God's "book" before one of them came to be (Ps. 139:16). Herod and Pilate did what God's "plan had predestined to take place" (Acts 4:28). And God "chose us" in Christ "before the foundation of the world" (Eph. 1:4). This doctrine of God's eternal decree is a great mystery and beyond our full comprehension. It is also a great comfort, for it means there are no surprises to God. No matter what difficulties we face in life, we are secure in our Father's hands. The same God and Father who prepared a kingdom for us "from the foundation of the world" (Matt. 25:34) has also numbered the hairs of our heads, so we need not fear (10:29–31).

THE ETERNAL FIRE OF HELL. Jesus teaches that on the final day those who reject him will face eternal punishment (25:41, 46), and Scripture elsewhere emphasizes the reality of eternal punishment for the wicked (Isa. 66:24; Dan. 12:2; Rev. 14:9–11). While some argue that the wicked are annihilated, the church affirms that their condemnation is permanent and ongoing, parallel to the eternal life of the righteous. This is supported by Jesus' teaching that judgment will vary based on one's deeds (Matt. 16:27), which would not apply if the wicked simply ceased to exist. This sobering truth calls for repentance and faith.

Personal Implications

Take time to reflect on the implications of Matthew 24:31–46 for your own life today. Consider what you have learned that might lead you to praise God, repent of sin, and trust in his gracious promises. Make notes below on the personal implications for your walk with the Lord of the (1) *Gospel Glimpses*, (2) *Whole-Bible Connections*, (3) *Theological Soundings*, and (4) the passage as a whole.

1. Gospel Glimpses

2. Whole-Bible Connections

3. Theological Soundings

4. Matthew 24:31–46

As You Finish This Unit . . .

Take a moment now to ask for the Lord's blessing and help as you continue in this study of Jesus' speech on the Mount of Olives. As you reflect on Jesus' promises for the future and what they mean for the present, pray, especially, that the "God of hope" might "fill you with all joy and peace in believing, so that by the power of the Holy Spirit you may abound in hope" (Rom. 15:13).

Definitions

[1] **The devil** – A spiritual being whose name *Satan* (Matt. 4:10) means "accuser." As the leader of all the demonic forces, he opposes God's rule and seeks to harm God's people and accuse them of wrongdoing. His power, however, is confined to the bounds that God has set for him, and one day he will be destroyed along with all his demons (Matt. 25:41; Rev. 20:10).

WEEK 10: JESUS' PROMISE ACCORDING TO MARK

Mark 13:1–37

The Place of the Passage

The Gospels of Mark and Luke also record Jesus' speech on the Mount of Olives. The next two studies focus on these parallel accounts. Like Matthew, Mark locates Jesus' speech after Jesus has made his final journey to Jerusalem, entered the city, overturned the tables in the temple, and engaged with the Jerusalem leadership (Mark 10–12). It is his second major speech in Mark: in the first he explained that God's kingdom has begun to arrive in his own life and work (4:1–34); now he explains that God's kingdom will arrive in all its fullness only when he returns in glory (13:1–37). Jesus is seated on the Mount of Olives and speaks "privately" with "Peter and James and John and Andrew" in response to their question about the destruction of the temple (13:1–4). Although their question confuses the temple's demise with the final consummation (13:4; cf. Dan. 12:7), Jesus himself distinguishes the two. He first addresses the question of *what* to expect (A and B) and then the question of *when* the prophesied events will occur (A' and B'). This gives the speech the following structure:

Introduction: Jesus' prophecy and the disciples' question (13:1–4)
(A) What: "These things" concerning the temple's destruction (13:5–23)
(B) What: The "coming" of the "Son of Man" (13:24–27)

(A') When: "These things" within a generation[1] (13:28–31)
(B') When: "That day" unknown (13:32–37)

The Big Picture

In Mark 13 Jesus prepares his disciples for the future: God's judgment on Jerusalem within a generation and—beyond that—God's final, universal, judgment when Jesus comes again in glory.

Reflection and Discussion

Read through the complete passage for this study, Mark 13:1–37. Then think through and write your own notes on the following questions. (For further background see the *ESV Study Bible*, pages 1922–1926, or visit esv.org.)

As in Matthew 24–25, Jesus delivers his speech in response to the disciples' question, "When will these things be, and what will be the sign when all these things are about to be accomplished?" (Mark 13:4). The disciples seem to conflate the destruction of Jerusalem with the end itself. In Mark 13:1–4, 7–8, 13 how does Jesus help us to distinguish "these things" from "the end"?

Mark specifies that it was "Peter and James and John and Andrew" who asked Jesus the question on the Mount of Olives and who heard his reply (Mark 13:3; cf. Matt. 24:3). In Mark Peter functions as a leader among the disciples (e.g., Mark 3:16; 8:29; 10:28; 14:29, 37; 16:7), and Peter, James, and John appear as an inner circle within the twelve (1:16–20; 5:37; 9:2; 14:33). Why might Mark have particularly noted that it was these three, together with Andrew (Peter's brother), who heard Jesus' speech? How does this give us confidence in the Gospel reports of Jesus' words?

In Mark 13:5–23 Jesus surveys the whole period between his present and "the end" (13:7, 13), that is, between his resurrection and return. After reading verses 5–13 and 21–23, list the events that will characterize the whole period until "the end." What challenges does Jesus prophesy that his followers will face? What encouragements does he provide amid these challenges?

In Mark 13:14–20 Jesus focuses on one crucial event within this period: the destruction of Jerusalem and its temple, which will occur in AD 70. He commands his disciples that, when they see these events approaching, they should "flee" Jerusalem and "pray" for God's mercy (13:14, 18). But if God is sovereign over history, as Jesus' prophecy makes clear, why pray? How can we hold together God's absolutely sovereignty and his command to pray for mercy in our trials?

In Mark 13:24–27 Jesus focuses on his own return as the "Son of Man." He indicates this new topic in three ways: (1) by using the conjunction "but" (13:24); (2) by speaking of a new period of time, namely "those days, after that tribulation" (13:24); and (3) by universalizing his language (contrast "when you see," 13:14, with "then they will see," 13:26). With this distinction in mind look back at Mark 13:5–13: How are faithful disciples meant to use this period of grace between the judgment of Jerusalem and the final judgment when Jesus returns?

In announcing his return Jesus applies several Old Testament prophecies to himself. Read each of the passages in the table below in its context. Since Jesus applies these texts to his own future, what does this teach us about his identity and about the purpose and character of his return?

	Old Testament	Jesus' Identity	Jesus' Return
Mark 13:24–25	Isaiah 13:10; 34:4 Joel 2:10; 3:14–15		
Mark 13:26	Daniel 7:13–14		
Mark 13:27	Deuteronomy 30:4 Zechariah 2:6–13		

In Mark 13:28–32 Jesus distinguishes the destruction of Jerusalem from his own return and explains how the two events are related. On the one hand Jesus refers to the destruction of Jerusalem as "all these things" that will "take place" within a generation (13:29–30 with 13:4). On the other hand Jesus refers to his return as the "Son of Man" as "that day an hour" about which "no one knows" (13:32 with 13:24–27). What do these two events have in common? How are they different?

Jesus concludes his speech by warning "all" to "be on guard" and "stay awake" (13:33, 37). This warning applies not only to the four disciples with Jesus on the Mount of Olives (13:5, 9, 23) but to "all" who will live between his resurrection and return, including us. How does the parable of the man on a journey (13:33–36) teach us what it means to "be on guard" and "stay awake" until Jesus returns?

Read through the following three sections on *Gospel Glimpses, Whole-Bible Connections*, and *Theological Soundings*. Then take time to consider the *Personal Implications* these sections have for you.

Gospel Glimpses

FOR THE SAKE OF THE ELECT. Jesus' remarkable statement in Mark 13:20 emphasizes God's sovereignty in saving his people: "the Lord . . . cut short the days . . . for the sake of the elect." The Lord knows those whom he has chosen, and in his sovereign grace he works out his purposes in history to ensure their salvation. In the period of the old covenant, even when God sent his judgment on Israel for their sin, he always preserved for himself a "remnant" (e.g., Isa. 11:11; Ezra 9:8, 13–15). So also, when God established his new covenant in Christ, he preserved for himself a remnant among the Jews, even as Jerusalem came under his judgment. God's chosen people among the Jews, who put their faith in Jesus, were spared the judgment (Mark 13:20) and so were able to take "the gospel . . . to all nations" (13:10). In this way God's "elect"—both Jews and Gentiles who trust in Christ—come to find salvation in his name.

Whole-Bible Connections

GATHERED FROM THE FOUR WINDS. Jesus' promise that he will "send out the angels and gather his elect" (13:27) indicates both that he will act as God when he comes to gather his people and that none of his people will be missing. His words echo the Lord's promise in Deuteronomy and Zechariah to "come," "gather" his people, and "dwell" in their "midst" on the final "day" (Deut. 30:4; Zech. 2:6, 10). In both prophecies it is the Lord—God himself—who acts, and Jesus applies both to his *own* future. Moreover, this final gathering will include *all* "*his* elect," for God's people belong *to him*. Jesus' unusual expression—"from the four winds, from the ends of the earth to the ends of heaven"—combines Zechariah's prophecy of the Lord's coming to gather his people (Zech. 2:6) from "many nations" (Zech. 2:11) with other biblical expressions of universality (e.g., Deut. 30:4; Neh. 1:9; Ps. 19:6; Jer. 12:12). Indeed, Jesus' prophecy further implies that "the angels" will gather both the living (on earth) and the dead (in heaven), so that none of God's people will be missing (cf. 1 Thess. 4:13–18).

Theological Soundings

THE FUTURE OF CREATION. Jesus' words in Mark 13:24–25, 31 may seem to suggest the destruction of the cosmos, but Scripture indicates God's plan is to renew and glorify creation, not annihilate it. The Old Testament covenant with Noah affirms God's ongoing commitment to the earth (Gen. 8:20–22; 9:7–17). In the New Testament Jesus speaks of the "renewal of all things" (Matt. 19:28), and Paul teaches that creation will be freed from corruption (Rom. 8:21). Peter likens future judgment by fire to the flood (2 Pet. 3:6–7), and Revelation speaks of God's making "all things new" (Rev. 21:5). These passages reveal that creation will be transformed, not destroyed, similar to Jesus' resurrected body. Mark 13:24–25 uses apocalyptic imagery to describe this radical change, while Mark 13:31 emphasizes the eternal authority of Jesus' words. Ultimately God plans a radical renewal, bringing forth a "new heavens and a new earth" (2 Pet. 3:13).

PRAYER AND GOD'S SOVEREIGNTY. If God is sovereign over the events of history, why pray? Why do anything? Jesus sees no contradiction between these two realities. He prophesies the destruction of Jerusalem (Mark 13:14) and the salvation of the elect (13:20) while also commanding his disciples to "flee" and to "pray" (13:14, 18). God's sovereignty is such that he works out his perfect plan in and through the prayers and actions of his people. So why pray? Because prayer is the means that God has appointed to bring about his perfect plan. The better question, then, is this: How can we not pray?

Personal Implications

Take time to reflect on the implications of Mark 13:1–37 for your own life today. Consider what you have learned that might lead you to praise God, repent of sin, and trust in his gracious promises. Make notes below on the personal implications for your walk with the Lord of the (1) *Gospel Glimpses*, (2) *Whole-Bible Connections*, (3) *Theological Soundings*, and (4) the passage as a whole.

1. Gospel Glimpses

2. Whole-Bible Connections

3. Theological Soundings

4. Mark 13:1–37

As You Finish This Unit . . .

Take a moment now to ask for the Lord's blessing and help as you continue in this study of Jesus' speech on the Mount of Olives. As you reflect on Jesus' promises for the future and what they mean for the present, pray, especially, that the "God of hope" might "fill you with all joy and peace in believing, so that by the power of the Holy Spirit you may abound in hope" (Rom. 15:13).

Definitions

[1] **Generation** – Jesus' reference to "this generation" (Mark 13:30) has been interpreted in various ways but most straightforwardly refers to Jesus' own contemporaries. This is the most common meaning of the noun "generation" (Greek *genea*) in the New Testament and early Christian literature. It also makes best sense of Mark's usage in its four other occurrences (8:12 [2x]; 8:38; 9:19).

Week 11: Jesus' Promise according to Luke

Luke 21:5–38

The Place of the Passage

The Gospel of Luke locates Jesus' speech after Jesus has entered Jerusalem, dramatically enacted the destruction of the temple, and engaged with the city's corrupt leadership (Luke 19:28–21:4). Jerusalem's leaders fail to recognize God's coming to them in Jesus (19:44; 20:13, 41–44), and they will soon face judgment for their various sins (19:41–44; 20:9–19; 20:45–21:4; cf. 13:1–9, 31–35). Luke does not draw attention to Jesus' location on the Mount of Olives (contrast Matt. 24:3 // Mark 13:3), but he does—like Matthew and Mark—record Jesus' prophecy of the destruction of the temple (Luke 21:6; cf. Matt. 24:2 // Mark 13:2) and the disciples' question, "When will these things be, and what will be the sign?" (Luke 21:7). As in Matthew and Mark, Jesus again distinguishes between "these things" that will lead to the destruction of Jerusalem "within a generation" (21:6–7, 9, 28, 31–32) and the "coming of the Son of Man" for final judgment at the end (21:25–28, 34–36). Luke in fact presents Jesus' speech as three smaller speeches (see 21:8, 10, 29) in which Jesus three times surveys the whole period from his present to "the end."

The Big Picture

In Luke 21 Jesus warns his disciples of the suffering to come, and he prepares them—and us—to be ready for his own return as the Son of Man.

Reflection and Discussion

Read through the complete passage for this study, Luke 21:5–38. Then think through and write your own notes on the following questions. (For further background see the *ESV Study Bible*, pages 2002–2004, or visit esv.org.)

In his first speech Jesus surveys briefly the whole period between his present and "the end" (Luke 21:8–9). He warns against false christs, who will claim that "the time is at hand," and he urges his followers to recognize that "the end will not be at once" (cf. 19:11). Why is it important—still today—to beware of false christs who claim "I am he" and "the time is at hand"?

In his second speech Jesus again surveys the whole period between his present and his final "coming" as the "Son of Man" (21:10–28). He first focuses on the period leading up to the destruction of Jerusalem (21:12–19) and warns that, although his disciples will face persecution (21:12, 16–17), this period is above all an "opportunity to bear witness" (21:13). Read Luke 24:44–49 and Acts 1:6–11 and note how these passages clarify the nature of the apostles' witness to Christ, specifically the substance (Bear witness about what?), scope (How far and wide? How long?), and strength (Who will enable them to bear witness?).

The Apostles' Witness	Substance	Scope	Strength
Luke 24:44–49			
Acts 1:6–11			

We are not Jesus' original disciples, but the task of bearing witness to him, in the power of the Holy Spirit, extends to the "end of the earth" and continues until his return (Acts 1:6–11). How is our role similar to that of the twelve apostles? How is our role different?

In Luke 21:12–15 Jesus warns his disciples that they will be put on trial for his sake, and he promises his own personal assistance: "I will give you a mouth and wisdom" (21:14–15). In the parallel in Mark 13:11 Jesus promises the assistance of the Holy Spirit. How similar or different are these two accounts of Jesus' promise? How does each provide comfort when we face pressure or persecution for Christ's sake?

In Luke 21:16 Jesus warns that "some" of his disciples will be "put to death" for his sake. In verse 18 he promises "not a hair of your head will perish." How can both these promises be true?

In Luke 21:24 Jesus speaks of the "times of the Gentiles [or "nations"]." Now read Luke 24:46–47 and Acts 1:7–8; 28:28. How do these passages clarify what these "times" involve, and why God has planned them?

How can we make the most of God's provision of these "times of the Gentiles"?

In Luke 21:25–28 Jesus looks forward to his own return. He clearly distinguishes the final "coming of the Son of Man" from the destruction of Jerusalem by (1) his reference to the "times of the Gentiles" (21:24), (2) his mention of that which is "coming on *the world*" (21:26; cf. 21:35), and (3) his description of the event itself. As in Matthew and Mark, Jesus uses language from several Old Testament passages (see table below) to indicate that the coming of the Son of Man will cause great cosmic upheaval. How do these passages clarify the nature and the scope of the final judgment?

	Who Judges?	Who Is Affected?
Ps. 46:1–7		
Ps. 65:5–8		
Isa. 13:1–13		
Isa. 24:17–23		
Ezek. 32:1–3, 7–8, 11–15		
Joel 2:28–3:2		
Hag. 2:6–7, 20–22		

In Luke 21:28–36 Jesus refers repeatedly to "these things" (21:28, 31) or "all these things" (21:32, 36). As in Matthew 24 and Mark 13, "these things" refer to the events leading up to and including the destruction of Jerusalem (see 21:6–7). From these verses how does Jesus teach us to live, now that "all these things" have in fact taken place and the next major event on God's calendar is the final judgment when Jesus returns?

Read through the following three sections on *Gospel Glimpses, Whole-Bible Connections*, and *Theological Soundings*. Then take time to consider the *Personal Implications* these sections have for you.

Gospel Glimpses

NOT A HAIR OF YOUR HEAD WILL PERISH. Jesus' warnings about persecution seem to contradict his promises of deliverance. "Some of you they will put to death," he says, "but not a hair of your head will perish" (Luke 21:16, 18). We need to take seriously both these words from our Lord. The first warns us that life will not necessarily be easy for his followers in the period between his resurrection and his return. The history of the church bears this out, and many of us can add testimony from our own experience. It is "through many tribulations" that "we must enter the kingdom of God" (Acts 14:22). And yet it is also true that "not a hair of your head will perish" (Luke 21:18). How can this be so? Only when we look to the resurrection. For our Lord Jesus, who himself suffered and died, was raised to new life in a body—in *his body*, the same body in which he died (24:31, 34, 36–43). Ultimately then not a hair of his head perished. In the same way, Jesus promises those who trust him that not a hair of our heads will perish. He will raise us bodily from the grave and enable us to "stand" before him at the end (21:27, 36).

Whole-Bible Connections

COMING IN A CLOUD. In Luke 21:27 Jesus declares that the "Son of Man" will come "in a cloud with power and great glory." The prophecy echoes Daniel 7:13 and parallels Matthew 24:31 and Mark 13:26, except for one subtle difference. Whereas Daniel, Matthew, and Mark include *plural* "clouds," in Luke Jesus focuses on only *one* of these clouds. His prophecy recalls the great coming of God at Mount Sinai, when the Lord came down on the mountain "in the [singular] cloud" (Ex. 34:5; cf. 19:16; 24:16). Luke has in fact already reminded us three times of that great event when he described how God appeared on the mountain at Jesus' transfiguration in a singular "cloud" and declared, "This is my Son" (Luke 9:34–35). Now, remarkably, Jesus announces that at the end *he* will come "in a cloud with power and great glory" (21:27; cf. Acts 1:9–11). Jesus' final "coming" as "the Son of Man" will be nothing less than the final coming of God himself.

Theological Soundings

THE VERY WORDS OF JESUS. Christians have always trusted the four canonical Gospels as God-given and reliable accounts of Jesus' life, death, and resurrection. However, since the eighteenth century some scholars have questioned their accuracy, focusing on differences between the accounts. The "quest for the historical Jesus" seeks to distinguish the "real" Jesus from the Gospel accounts, examining what Jesus "really" said. This approach, however, is misguided. The church has long acknowledged that the Gospels do not provide a bare, uninterpreted account of Jesus' life. They are Spirit-inspired, faithful interpretations of his life and teachings—the Gospel *according to* Matthew, Mark, Luke, and John. While the Gospels may focus on different words, the substance of Jesus' message is consistent across them. Just as we can faithfully retell a story without always focusing on the exact same elements, so the Gospel writers present the truth of Jesus' words and actions. Jesus promised that the Holy Spirit would help his apostles remember his teachings (John 14:26), ensuring that the Gospels faithfully represent his words for our salvation (2 Tim. 3:16).

Personal Implications

Take time to reflect on the implications of Luke 21:5–38 for your own life today. Consider what you have learned that might lead you to praise God, repent of sin, and trust in his gracious promises. Make notes below on the personal implications for your walk with the Lord of the (1) *Gospel Glimpses*, (2) *Whole-Bible Connections*, (3) *Theological Soundings*, and (4) the passage as a whole.

1. Gospel Glimpses

2. Whole-Bible Connections

3. Theological Soundings

4. Luke 21:5–38

As You Finish This Unit . . .

Take a moment now to ask for the Lord's blessing and help as you complete this study of Jesus' speech on the Mount of Olives. As you reflect on Jesus' promises for the future and what they mean for the present, pray, especially, that the "God of hope" might "fill you with all joy and peace in believing, so that by the power of the Holy Spirit you may abound in hope" (Rom. 15:13).

Week 12: Come, Lord Jesus!

1 Thessalonians 4–5; 2 Peter 3; Revelation 22

The Olivet Discourse outside the Gospels

Jesus' speech on the Mount of Olives had a huge impact on his apostles. It shaped the way they proclaimed the gospel and taught about the future in their letters. The themes and images of Jesus' speech are also repeated in the book of Revelation. In this final study we will examine two key passages from the apostles Paul (1 Thess. 4:13–5:11) and Peter (2 Pet. 3:1–18) in which they each repeat Jesus' promise to return and then apply it to the lives of Christian believers. We will also then consider briefly Jesus' promise to return in the book of Revelation (Rev. 22:6–21).

The Big Picture

The apostles repeat and reaffirm Jesus' promise to return and teach us how to live for him until we see him face to face.

Reflection and Discussion

Read through the first passage for this study, 1 Thessalonians 4:13–5:11. Then think through and write your own notes on the following questions. (For further background see the *ESV Study Bible*, pages 2309–2310, or visit esv.org.)

Paul's teaching about Jesus' return in 1 Thessalonians 4:13–5:11 contains several points of connection to Jesus' speech on the Mount of Olives. All three Synoptic Gospels are paralleled, but for the sake of simplicity we will focus on Matthew. Look up the following verses and note the parallels:

Jesus	Paul	Common Words or Images
Matt. 24:30–31	1 Thess. 4:16–17	
Matt. 24:42–44	1 Thess. 5:2	
Matt. 24:37–39	1 Thess. 5:3	
Matt. 24:42–43, 49	1 Thess. 5:6–8	

How does Paul use Jesus' teaching to warn about the coming judgment?

How does Paul use Jesus' teaching to comfort us and give us hope?

According to Paul how should we respond to Jesus' promise to return?

Read through the second passage for this study, 2 Peter 3:1–18. Then think through and write your own notes on the following questions. (For further background see the *ESV Study Bible*, pages 2422–2423.)

Peter's teaching about Jesus' return in 2 Peter 3:1–18 also contains several points of connection to Jesus' speech on the Mount of Olives. Again, all three Synoptic Gospels are paralleled here, but for the sake of simplicity we will focus on Matthew. Look up the following verses and note the parallels:

Jesus	Peter	Common Words or Images
Matt. 24:24–25	2 Pet. 3:2–3	
Matt. 24:37–39	2 Pet. 3:6	
Matt. 24:48; 25:5	2 Pet. 3:9	
Matt. 24:39, 42–44, 50	2 Pet. 3:10	
Matt. 24:35	2 Pet. 3:10	
Matt. 24:46	2 Pet. 3:10	
Matt. 24:50	2 Pet. 3:12–14	

How does Peter use Jesus' teaching to warn about the coming judgment?

How does Peter use Jesus' teaching to comfort us and give us hope?

According to Peter, how should we respond to Jesus' promise to return?

Read through the third passage for this study, Revelation 22:6–21. Then think through and write your own notes on the following questions. (For further background see the *ESV Study Bible*, pages 2496–2497.)

The book of Revelation opens and closes with promises of Jesus' return (Rev. 1:7; 22:20). At several points in the book the Lord himself declares that he is coming soon (2:5, 16; 3:3, 11, 20; 16:15; 22:7, 12, 20), often using words and images we recognize from Jesus' speech on the Mount of Olives (and other places in the Gospels). Once again, all three Synoptic Gospels are paralleled here, but for the sake of simplicity we will focus on Matthew. Look up the following verses and note the parallels.

Jesus	Revelation	Common Words or Images
Matt. 24:30–31	Rev. 1:7	
Matt. 24:42–44	Rev. 3:3–5; 16:15	
Matt. 24:33	Rev. 3:20–21	
Matt. 24:11, 24	Rev. 16:13–14	

Revelation closes with Jesus' thrice-stated promise "I am coming soon" (Rev. 22:7, 12, 20). How does this promise provide both warning and comfort? How do verses 6–21 encourage us to respond to our Lord's promise to return?

Read through the following three sections on *Gospel Glimpses*, *Whole-Bible Connections*, and *Theological Soundings*. Then take time to consider the *Personal Implications* these sections have for you.

Gospel Glimpses

GRIEVING WITH HOPE. Writing to the Thessalonians, Paul applies Jesus' promise to return to the problem of death (1 Thess. 4:13–18). He reminds them of a "word from the Lord" (1 Thess. 4:15), which reflects Jesus' promise to return, recorded in Matthew 24:30–31. "The Lord himself will descend from heaven," Paul affirms, and he will then gather his people—both the living and the dead—so that "we will always be with the Lord" (1 Thess. 4:16–17 with Matt. 24:30–31). This is indeed great comfort in the face of death. Our Lord Jesus, who himself died and rose again, "will bring with him those who have fallen asleep" (1 Thess. 4:14). So, although we rightly grieve when brothers and sisters in Christ die, we do "not grieve as others do who have no hope" (1 Thess. 4:13). We *grieve*, because death is an enemy—"the last enemy" (1 Cor. 15:26). But we grieve *with hope*, because our Lord has defeated death and, when he comes, will share that victory with all his people (1 Thess. 4:16–17; 1 Cor. 15:21–23). "Therefore," Paul urges us, "encourage one another with these words" (1 Thess. 4:18).

Whole-Bible Connections

THE TEACHING OF JESUS AND HIS APOSTLES. It should be no surprise to find echoes of Jesus' words in writings of his apostles. Jesus was their "Lord and Teacher" (John 13:13–14), and he promised them that, after his ascension, the Holy Spirit would remind them of all that he had said (John 14:26). While modern critical scholars have often attempted to drive a wedge between Jesus and the New Testament, we are right to see a very close connection between the two. Although we have Jesus' words mediated to us through the words of his apostles—both in the Gospels and in the Epistles and Revelation—the words of the New Testament *are* the words of our Lord. We are right therefore to receive them with thanks, to treasure them, and to live by them. As the apostle Peter said to Jesus when others were turning away, "Lord, to whom shall we go? You have the words of eternal life" (John 6:68).

Theological Soundings

COME, LORD JESUS. In the first of these studies we noted that, while the *center* of the gospel is Christ's death for our sins and resurrection as Lord (1 Cor. 15:3–5), the *climax* of the gospel is Jesus' promise to return (1 Cor. 15:20–28). In fact the return of Christ is the climax not only of the gospel but of the whole biblical story. From the very beginning God created us to live with him in his presence (Genesis 1–2). When our first parents sinned, God cast them out of his presence, but he did not give up on his plan to live with his people (see Genesis 3). The story of the Bible, then, is the story of God's coming to his people. He comes to dwell with Israel in the wilderness (Ex. 40:35–38) and in the Jerusalem temple (1 Kings 8:9–11). He comes to dwell *with us* in his Son (Matt 1:23; John 1:14) and *among us* and *within us* by his Spirit (John 14:23; Acts 2:38; 1 Cor. 3:16; 6:19). In the end, when Jesus returns, our God will come to dwell with us fully, and finally, and forever (Rev. 21:3). The return of Christ, then, is not an unimportant appendix to the Christian gospel but its climax and goal. It is therefore fitting that, when we hear our Lord's promise, "Surely, I am coming soon," we respond with the words given to us on the very last page of the Bible: "Amen. Come, Lord Jesus!" (Rev. 22:20).

Personal Implications

Take time to reflect on the implications of 1 Thessalonians 4–5; 2 Peter 3; and Revelation 22 for your own life today. Consider what you have learned that might lead you to praise God, repent of sin, and trust in his gracious promises. Make notes below on the personal implications for your walk with the Lord of the (1) *Gospel Glimpses*, (2) *Whole-Bible Connections*, (3) *Theological Soundings*, and (4) the passages as a whole.

1. Gospel Glimpses

2. Whole-Bible Connections

3. Theological Soundings

4. 1 Thessalonians 4–5; 2 Peter 3; Revelation 22

As You Finish Studying the Olivet Discourse . . .

We rejoice with you as you conclude this study! May the truths learned here become part of your daily walk with God. Now we would encourage you to continue to study the Word of God on a regular basis. To continue your study of the Bible, we would invite you to consider other books in the *Knowing the Bible* series, and to visit www.crossway.org/knowingthebible.

Lastly, take a moment to look back through this study. Review the notes that you have written, and the things that you have highlighted. Reflect again on the key themes that the Lord has been teaching you about himself. May these things become a treasure for you throughout your life—this we pray in the name of the Father, and the Son, and the Holy Spirit. Amen.

KNOWING THE BIBLE STUDY GUIDE SERIES

Experience the *Grace* of God in the *Word* of God

Series Volumes

- Genesis
- Exodus
- Leviticus
- Numbers
- Deuteronomy
- Joshua
- Judges
- Ruth and Esther
- 1–2 Samuel
- 1–2 Kings
- 1–2 Chronicles
- Ezra and Nehemiah
- Job
- Psalms
- Proverbs
- Ecclesiastes
- Song of Solomon
- Isaiah
- Jeremiah
- Lamentations, Habakkuk, and Zephaniah
- Ezekiel
- Daniel
- Hosea
- Joel, Amos, and Obadiah
- Jonah, Micah, and Nahum
- Haggai, Zechariah, and Malachi
- Matthew
- Mark
- Luke
- John
- Acts
- Romans
- 1 Corinthians
- 2 Corinthians
- Galatians
- Ephesians
- Philippians
- Colossians and Philemon
- 1–2 Thessalonians
- 1–2 Timothy and Titus
- Hebrews
- James
- 1–2 Peter and Jude
- 1–3 John
- Revelation
- The Parables of Jesus
- The Sermon on the Mount
- The Ten Commandments
- Jesus' Farewell Discourse
- Jesus' Speech on the Mount of Olives
- The Miracles of Jesus

crossway.org/knowingthebible